CIVIC UNREST

INVESTIGATE THE STRUGGLE FOR SOCIAL CHANGE

INQUIRE AND INVESTIGATE

Marcia Amidon Lusted
Illustrated by Lena Chandhok

Nomad Press
A division of Nomad Communications
10 9 8 7 6 5 4 3 2 1

This book was manufactured by Marquis Book Printing,
Montmagny Québec, Canada
March 2015, Job #109681
ISBN Softcover: 978-1-61930-245-7
ISBN Hardcover: 978-1-61930-241-9

Illustrations by Lena Chandhok
Educational Consultant, Marla Conn

Questions regarding the ordering of this book should be addressed to
Nomad Press
2456 Christian St.
White River Junction, VT 05001
www.nomadpress.net

Printed in Canada.

~ Titles in the Inquire and Investigate Series ~

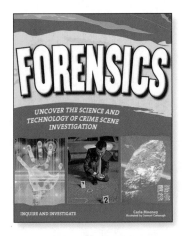

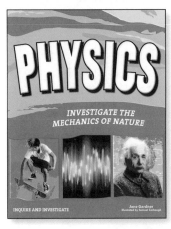

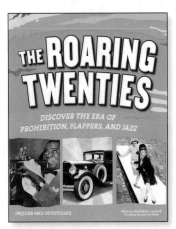

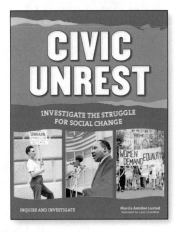

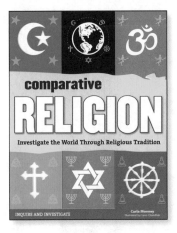

Interested in primary sources?

PS Look for this icon.

You can use a smartphone or tablet app to scan the QR codes and explore more about civic unrest! Cover up neighboring QR codes to make sure you're scanning the right one. You can find a list of each URL on the Resources page.

Contents

TIMELINE

507 BCE .... Cleisthenes creates a system of political reforms called "demokratia."

1768 CE .... Tailors strike in New York City, the earliest recorded strike in U.S. history.

1773, December 16 .... During the Boston Tea Party, colonists throw 90,000 pounds of British tea into Boston Harbor to protest a British tax on tea.

1774, July 4 .... Delegates to the Second Continental Congress sign the Declaration of Independence.

1775–1783 .... Americans fight the British in the American Revolutionary War.

1787 .... The Founding Fathers write the U.S. Constitution during the Constitutional Convention.

1789–1799 .... French peasants rise up against the aristocracy during the French Revolution.

1794 .... Shoemakers in Philadelphia form the first labor union.

1848 .... The first Women's Rights Convention is held in Seneca Falls, New York.

1858–1947 .... India is ruled by the British until India gains independence through campaigns of civic unrest, often led by Mahatma Gandhi.

1877 .... A coal miners' strike in Pennsylvania leads to the hanging of 19.

1894 .... Railroad porters organize the Pullman boycott and workers' strike.

1899–1902 .... In Colombia, liberals and conservatives fight each other in the War of a Thousand Days.

1909 .... Female textile workers in New York City go on strike to protest working conditions.

1910–1920 .... Revolutionaries fight the government in the Mexican Revolution.

1911, March 25 .... The Triangle Shirtwaist Fire in New York City kills 146 workers, most of them women.

1774, July 4

1909

TIMELINE

1914............................A coal miners' strike in Colorado leads to the deaths of 22 people.

1920............................The 19th Amendment gives women the right to vote.

1948–1994................South Africa suffers under the system of apartheid.

1948, January 30.......Mahatma Gandhi is assassinated.

1954–1968................African Americans and their supporters fight for equality during the Civil Rights movement.

1955, December 1......Rosa Parks refuses to give up her seat on the bus.

1963–1990................Nelson Mandela is imprisoned in South Africa.

1968, April 4..............Reverend Martin Luther King Jr. is assassinated.

1989, April–June........The Tiananmen Square protests take place in Beijing, China.

1989, June 5..............."Tank Man" stands up to Chinese tanks on their way to Tiananmen Square.

1999, November 30...Protests against the World Trade Organization take place in Seattle, Washington.

2010............................The Arab Spring begins with protests in Tunisia.

2011, September 17...The Occupy Wall Street movement begins in New York City.

2012, October 9.........Malala Yousafzai is shot in the head by a member of the Taliban as she travels home from school in Pakistan.

2013............................The struggle over democracy and Russian annexation begins in Ukraine.

2014, December 15....One million workers across Indonesia go on strike to demand higher wages.

2014............................Social media plays a major role in informing the public that protests in Ferguson, Missouri, have erupted after Michael Brown is shot and killed by a white police officer.

1909

1989, April 15–June 5

Introduction ▶

What Is Civic Unrest?

IT'S MY CIVIC DUTY!

I VOTED

What do we mean when we talk about civic unrest? What is the connection between civic unrest and democracy?

FORMAL DEMOCRACY STARTED WITH THE GREEKS...

...AND EVENTUALLY SPREAD...

...TO COUNTRIES ALL OVER THE WORLD.

Civic unrest is disruption for the sake of bringing awareness to specific causes. It can involve demonstrations, marches, communication of discontent. Civic unrest can sometimes be violent. Can you think of examples of civic unrest happening today?

On December 1, 1955, Rosa Parks refused to give up her seat on a Montgomery city bus in Montgomery, Alabama. Her feet hurt after a long day of working as a seamstress, but that wasn't the only reason she stayed sitting.

At the time that Rosa Parks refused to move, buses were divided into two sections. There was one section for white people and one for black people. When the white section filled up, the bus driver ordered Parks to stand so a white man could take her seat in the black section. She refused, and was later arrested and convicted of violating the laws of segregation. These laws were enacted to keep black people separate from white people.

Rosa Parks was practicing a nonviolent form of civic unrest. She was disrupting the usual flow of business to bring awareness to the fact that the rules of the bus were unfair.

Civic unrest can be violent or peaceful, organized or chaotic. Civic unrest can be as simple as writing a letter to the editor of the newspaper, or as complicated as calling on thousands of people to march in different cities all over the world.

Through civic unrest, Rosa Parks galvanized the civil rights movement and changed the lives of people for generations to come. She has become known as the "first lady of civil rights." While civil rights had been on the minds of American citizens before Parks kept her seat, the movement was galvanized by Parks' calm refusal in the face of racist laws. The movement was influenced by a few of this country's greatest leaders, including Martin Luther King Jr.

Here in the United States, we live in a democracy. The most important element of democracy is the premise that power rests with the people. This means that a country's citizens determine who leads their government.

There is another critical aspect of democracy that Americans make great use of every day.

> Built into the U.S. Constitution are certain rights—freedom of speech, freedom of the press, freedom of religion, the right to public assembly, and the right to protest.

The People Say

"Democracy . . . is a charming form of government, full of variety and disorder; and dispensing a sort of equality to equals and unequals alike."

—Plato, ancient Greek philosopher

Through public planning, communication, and gatherings, citizens of democracies can change how their countries operate.

Rosa Parks was practicing these rights when she refused to give up her seat. These rights mean that anyone can engage in civic unrest. Have you ever written a letter or email to the president, a newspaper, or your principal in protest of something? Have you ever gone on a march to bring awareness to a certain issue?

If so, you were engaging in civic unrest. Civic unrest is an ongoing process of change.

SEEDS OF CHANGE

Because they live in a democracy, Americans are able to speak out against practices they believe are unfair. Citizens in countries all over the world are striving to reach this level of freedom and democratic rule.

People who do not live in a democracy sometimes face a government that has absolute control over their lives. Rulers in these countries rarely have to justify their actions, and ordinary citizens have very little say in how their countries are run. In some of these countries, the struggle for democracy is in evidence every day.

Around the world today, people are engaged in protests and demonstrations. They are attempting to gain the right to vote, to work to support their families, to receive an education, to speak freely, and to be treated with fairness.

Sometimes civic unrest can even lead to revolution. The American Revolution in the 1700s and the more recent Arab Spring are examples of civic unrest sparking revolution and dramatic change.

People also practice civic unrest in protest of social practices they believe are unfair. In the United States and around the world, people have protested and continue to work against the inhumane treatment suffered by minorities, women, and laborers.

Have you heard of the Occupy Wall Street movement? This movement was led by people who felt it is unfair that a small percentage of people control the majority of the world's wealth. Their protest may not have led to any lasting change, but it did bring attention to the issue and raise awareness.

The practice of civic unrest is much different today than 100 years ago. Advances in technology make it possible to see what's happening on the other side of the world at the moment it's happening. People who feel passionately about a topic can come together through websites and social media to join forces. Citizens also have more access to politicians than ever, which can have both positive and negative consequences.

While the methods of civic unrest might adapt to fit the decade, the passion and conviction of people who choose to protest are familiar across time and space.

By refusing to give up her seat, Rosa Parks prompted a movement that affected an entire country. That one small act of civic unrest led to an enormous change.

[
What are you passionate about?
What are you going to do to change
the world?
]

Chapter 1

Democracy in the United States

Why is democracy such an important form of government?

In a democracy, people are free to participate in their government and determine who is going to lead them. It gives power to the people, not the leaders.

Civic LESSON

The oldest written constitution in the world, which is still used to govern, is the Massachusetts state constitution. Written in 1780, it is older than the U.S. Constitution by eight years.

Democracy as a system of government dates back to the time of the ancient Greeks. Some historians think democracy is even older than that, but the Greeks were the first civilization to make democracy their official way of life.

In 507 BCE, a leader named Cleisthenes in Athens, Greece, created a system of political reforms that he called demokratia. Cleisthenes's demokratia only lasted for 200 years in Athens, but it has remained one of the Greeks' greatest contributions to the world.

Since its founding in 1776, the government of the United States has operated on a structure very similar to the ancient Greek demokratia. American citizens elect representatives to vote for them in Washington, DC. These elected representatives form the legislative branch, which makes our laws.

RULING BY RIGHT, RULING BY FORCE

A democracy provides citizens with rights that give them many opportunities and freedoms. These rights encourage them to contribute their voices to the ongoing conversation about how their government operates. Citizens choose who represents them. Citizens can help develop their laws and protest against the things they disagree with. Democracy is about the power of people.

[How does democracy compare to other forms of government?]

It used to be that the power to rule came by two different paths. In a monarchy, the path is heredity, which is when a royal family of monarchs hands the right to rule down to their children. The other path is through sheer force, when wars and other military actions decide who wins the right to rule. This is called a dictatorship. A dictator rules over a country with total control over everything.

In the monarchies of today, the royal family is usually a figurehead of the government. It holds very little real power. The actual ruling of the country is done by a legislative body, such as a parliament, headed by a prime minister or other political leader. This is known as a constitutional monarchy. The power of the royal family is limited by a written constitution and it has little or no political power.

The word *democracy* never appears in the U.S. Constitution.

WHO IS A CITIZEN?

In ancient Athens, the definition of citizen was very narrow and did not include women, slaves, or foreigners. Only men over the age of 18 with Athenian parents could be citizens. Originally the United States had a limited definition of citizen, much as the ancient Athenians did. But with time we have made amendments to our Constitution to allow people of all races and both genders to vote. A person born to an American citizen is automatically a citizen, but many other people are able to become citizens each year.

Great Britain is a familiar example of a constitutional monarchy. The queen of England has very little real power, though she is a well-respected symbol of the country and its history.

Totalitarian countries, dictatorships, and communism may seem like similar governmental structures, but they're actually very different. Communism is an economic system—the government owns all manner of production and the products. No one person is allowed to own any one thing. If you lived in a communist country, you wouldn't be allowed to own your bike and the government could take it any time it wanted.

In a dictatorship, one person is in charge. A dictator is a ruler with total control over a country, and this person has often gotten this power through intimidation and force. Cuba is an example of a dictatorship country. If you lived in Cuba, you might not be allowed to hear news from other parts of the world, or even news stories from your own city.

Totalitarian governments are similar to dictatorships because the ruler has control over everything, including its citizens' economic and political activities. However, a totalitarian government goes a step further and controls even its citizens' private lives.

Totalitarian governments usually have an overall belief or political ideology. For example, the Nazi regime in the 1930s and 1940s was a totalitarian government that believed that one race of people was superior to all others. Totalitarian governments can be run by a single dictator or by a group of rulers.

A DEMOCRACY IS A REPUBLIC

The United States, like most modern democracies, is actually a republic. In a republic, people don't take a direct role in legislation or governing. Voters don't head to the polls every time a new bill is introduced. Instead, they elect leaders who do this for them.

The ancient Greek philosopher Aristotle thought that a pure democracy, in which everyone voted on everything, was not actually the best way to rule a country. He thought that government run by the masses would lead to disorder or lawlessness. Do you think he was right? Why or why not?

Modern democracies also have agreements or formal understandings between the people and their government. The most common form of this written agreement is a constitution, which defines and limits what a government can and can't do. It also supplies procedures for how things should be done.

Some modern democracies, such as Great Britain, have unwritten constitutions. These are based on customs and laws that have been established through time.

> When a government is meeting the needs of its citizens, people are willing to follow the laws, because they know they have the power to replace their leaders if their government breaks this trust.

A true democracy has elections in which there are multiple candidates for each position. People vote by secret ballot so they don't have to worry about negative consequences for voting for the "wrong" candidate.

Some governments may look like democracies from the outside, but do not actually operate as democracies. Before the breakup of the Soviet Union in 1991, several of the communist countries of Eastern Europe seemed like democracies. Sometimes they even referred to themselves as "people's republics." Many of these countries had written constitutions. Their government structure included a legislature to pass laws, and they even held elections.

However, a few top Communist officials held most of the power. Everyone beneath them simply approved their decisions with only the appearance of democratic rule. These so-called democracies often had elections that were directed, meaning that voters were offered a choice of only one candidate, or the government controlled the campaign so that it couldn't be defeated.

LIFE, LIBERTY, AND THE PURSUIT OF HAPPINESS

Perhaps the most valuable indicators of a true democracy are the freedoms granted each citizen—beyond the power of choice in how he or she is ruled. In America's Declaration of Independence, in which the colonies of America set forth their desire in 1776 to be free from British rule, the country's founders wrote:

We hold these truths to be self-evident, that all men are created equal, that they are endowed by their Creator with certain unalienable Rights, that among these are Life, Liberty and the pursuit of Happiness.

> The writers weren't saying that people simply had the right to live. They also wanted people to be independent and to have the freedom to fully engage in activities that make for a happier society.

Later, the writers of the U.S. Constitution created a specific section called the Bill of Rights. It is the Bill of Rights that outlines the rights of the citizens of the United States. The Bill of Rights consists of the first 10 amendments to the U.S. Constitution.

Some of these amendments deal with the rights of citizens to keep and bear arms, to be safe from unlawful searches and seizures, and to have speedy trials in criminal court cases. The first amendment to the U.S. Constitution outlines many rights, including the right to free speech and to freely practice civic unrest.

THE FOUR FREEDOMS

One of artist Norman Rockwell's best known works is a series of paintings called "The Four Freedoms," in which the freedoms of speech and worship and freedom from fear and want are illustrated in images of regular Americans living their daily lives. You can view the four paintings here.

WHAT IS A CONSTITUTION?

A constitution is a written set of guidelines and procedures. It states how a country's government will be organized and run and how its people will behave.

> A constitution does not actually contain the rules. Instead it defines how rules will be decided, how they will be enforced, and who will interpret what they mean.

If a constitution actually included all of the laws and rules of a country, it would be unwieldy and constantly in need of updating. A good constitution shouldn't need to be changed very often because it creates a framework, or a basic plan. This framework defines procedures, such as how laws will be enacted and how the government will be run, and the overall rights of its citizens.

A constitution separates an unlimited democracy from a constitutional democracy. There are limits on the power of the majority rule in a constitutional democracy. Even though the people have the right to choose who will govern and how, restrictions are put in place so that a large and powerful group of people cannot get their way simply through large numbers. This might result in the rights of other people being violated.

DRAFTING THE CONSTITUTION

When the Founding Fathers gathered together in Philadelphia in May 1787 for the Constitutional Convention, they had a huge task in front of them. They had to write a constitution that would rule a very large country, a country that would only grow bigger.

CONSTITUTION CONFLICT

James Madison wrote a letter to Thomas Jefferson in 1788: "Wherever the real power in a Government lies, there is the danger of oppression. In our Governments, the real power lies in the majority of the Community, and the invasion of private rights is chiefly to be apprehended, not from acts of Government contrary to the sense of its constituents, but from acts in which the Government is the mere instrument of the major number [majority] of the constituents."

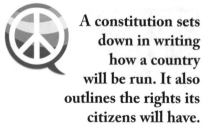

A constitution sets down in writing how a country will be run. It also outlines the rights its citizens will have.

The Constitution had to be ratified by nine out of the 13 colonies to be considered a law. Five colonies ratified it quickly in December 1787. It took another seven months, plus the promise of amendments, for enough colonies to ratify the document. Ten months later, the new government structure was in place.

The writers of the Constitution made many important decisions. They officially named the country "The United States of America." More importantly, they agreed to structure the government in three parts—the legislative, executive, and judicial branches.

The legislative branch includes the lawmaking bodies of Congress, which are divided into the House of Representatives and the Senate. The executive branch consists of the president. And the judicial branch is made up of a hierarchy of courts, from local courts all the way up to the Supreme Court.

These three branches were created to cover the areas of government. They also provide a system of checks and balances, so that no one branch can hold more power than the others. The Constitution itself is more powerful than any of the three branches. The writers of the Constitution wanted to guarantee basic human rights and freedoms and to provide a government by the consent of the governed.

CiViC LESSON

Even though the United States fought the British for independence in the American Revolution, the Founding Fathers drew inspiration for the Bill of Rights in the U.S. Constitution from the English Bill of Rights of 1689.

CONSTITUTION BOOGIE

Listen to a rap song about the Constitution. How does music help us remember historical facts?

America's constitution is still effective more than 200 years after it was written, something very few other countries can claim.

The Constitution can be changed if circumstances call for it. Amendments have been added for specific reasons, such as adding voting rights for women and people of color.

However, amendments cannot be added easily. Since 1789, there have been more than 11,000 amendments suggested for the Constitution. Only 27 have actually been approved.

U.S. ELECTIONS

Have you ever visited the polls on voting day? In the United States, elections are held on the Tuesday following the first Monday in November. Elections are in even-numbered years for congressional positions, and in odd-numbered years for some state and local positions.

All 435 representatives in the House of Representatives are elected every two years. Senators serve staggered terms of six years each, so in each election only about one-third of the Senators are elected. Every four years, a president and vice president are elected. Why do you think the Founding Fathers decided on staggered terms of office?

There are two types of elections in the United States: primary and general elections. A primary is an election that draws from a large pool of candidates and decides the ones who will represent their political parties in the general election. The presidential and vice-presidential candidates for each political party have usually been chosen at the party's convention the previous summer. The convention choice usually confirms the choices made by voters during the state primaries.

FIVE FREEDOMS EXPLAINED

There are five specific parts of the First Amendment that guarantee Americans some of their most cherished rights:

Congress shall make no law respecting an establishment of religion, or prohibiting the free exercise thereof; or abridging the freedom of speech, or of the press; or the right of the people peaceably to assemble, and to petition the Government for a redress of grievances.

These are called the Five Freedoms: the freedom of religion, freedom of speech, freedom of the press, the freedom to assemble peacefully, and the freedom to petition the government.

THE DONKEY IS THE SYMBOL OF THE DEMOCRATIC PARTY.

THE ELEPHANT IS THE SYMBOL OF THE REPUBLICAN PARTY.

In some countries, members of the media live in fear of arrest or attack for reporting on events.

These five freedoms may seem unremarkable to citizens of the United States after living under the Constitution for more than 200 years. But for people in other parts of the world, or for people who come to America from countries with other forms of governments, these freedoms are extremely important.

Freedom of religion was especially important to the Founding Fathers in writing the Constitution. From the beginning, America was a place where many people came so they could practice their religion without the fear of being persecuted. This freedom also meant that the government could not establish an official religion and expect its citizens to follow it.

Freedom of speech gives Americans the right to speak out and express their opinions without worrying that the government will interfere or punish them as a result. Have you ever read the editorial section of your local newspaper? In countries without freedom of speech, writing opinions is against the law.

> Freedom of the press is closely related to freedom of speech, because it allows the press–including newspapers, magazines, websites, books, and blogs–to publish news, information, and opinions without being censored.

Freedom of the press also includes the rights of regular citizens to publish their own newspapers, magazines, and newsletters under the same protections as official publishers. If you publish a family newsletter, you can print anything you want without getting in trouble with the government because of freedom of the press.

In addition to the right to share their opinions, both verbally and in writing, Americans may also gather together in groups to support their causes. They can collect in public places to express themselves or educate others about their causes. They can carry signs, march, demonstrate, protest, and express themselves in almost any way that is peaceful and nonviolent.

The People's Climate March in New York City in 2014 was the largest climate march in history, attended by more than 400,000 people. This march was possible because of the freedom to gather in groups to support a cause.

The freedom of petition is another important part of civic unrest. In many places around the world, speaking out against the government can lead to imprisonment or even death. But in the United States, citizens have a guaranteed freedom to tell their government what they like and don't like, and what they want to change. They can appeal to the government in favor of or against certain policies that affect them or that they feel strongly about. They can gather signatures on petitions and lobby their government representatives.

Americans might take these freedoms for granted. Attending the church of one's choice, writing a letter to the editor of the local paper, emailing a congressional representative about a pending bill, or speaking up at a town meeting to express an opinion are all examples of these five freedoms. But sometimes, practicing these freedoms involves a larger, louder effort.

ELECTORAL COLLEGE

American voters do not directly vote for the president and vice president. Instead, they vote for a group of electors in each state, who are pledged to vote for one candidate or the other. It's a "winner takes all" situation in most states—the votes of all the electors in a state go to the candidate who received the most popular votes in that state. For a candidate to become president, he or she must have an absolute majority of the 538 electoral votes in the electoral college.

In 1824, 1876, 1888, and 2000, the president won the electoral vote but did not win the popular vote.

KEY QUESTIONS

- How does the U.S. Constitution protect Americans' right to civic unrest?

- How do we make sure elections are fair in the United States? Why is this important?

YOU, THE CANDIDATE

An election for a school class president can be democracy in action!

- Choose two people from your class or group to play the parts of candidates for class president. Each candidate will have two minutes to present a speech about why they should be president.

- Then both students will have five minutes to debate with each other. The candidates can ask each other questions and try to show that he or she is the best qualified.

- Give students an opportunity to ask questions of each candidate. Each candidate should have the chance to respond to each question.

- After the speeches and debates, the class votes on the candidates. Then discuss what made each person choose their vote. What was it about each candidate that was persuasive? What wasn't persuasive?

To investigate more, write an editorial from each of two viewpoints. One is that of a student who wants to be class president so he or she can write about the role on their college applications. The other candidate is sincerely interested in making changes in the school. For each viewpoint, be as persuasive as possible. Ask a teacher or a friend to decide which editorial is more effective.

READ ALL ABOUT IT!

On November 3, 1948, the headline on the *Chicago Tribune* read "DEWEY DEFEATS TRUMAN," but the newspaper had gone to print before the election results for all states were reported. Democrat Harry Truman was the actual winner of the presidency. You can see the headline here.

I'M BETTER QUALIFIED!

BUT I'M MORE LIKEABLE!

WHO DECIDES?

Imagine that your school is going to choose a new mascot. A mascot is an important symbol of the pride and dedication students feel for their school, and it's important to choose an image that expresses those feelings. What is the best way for this choice to be made?

- **Divide your group into three smaller groups.** One group represents the executive branch, one is the judicial branch, and one is the legislative branch.

- **Each group makes a list as to why it is best suited for choosing the mascot.** What about the group's knowledge and experience makes it best qualified to choose? Are any of the groups in danger of being biased in any way?

- **Have all three groups come together to make their cases.** How can each argue why it should be chosen to decide on a new mascot?

- **Together, make a decision.** Decide if one group should be given this job, or if it should be a combination of either two of the groups or all three. Do all three groups working together result in a better decision for everyone?

To investigate more, consider how this process compares to the process that our three branches of government follow when the United States makes a decision. What are the advantages and disadvantages to a single group deciding, or of all three groups deciding?

WHO'S IN CHARGE?

What would your life be like if you were governed by someone who didn't follow the rules or made up his or her own rules? Here's your chance to find out!

- **Have everyone in the classroom or in your family put their names on slips of paper.** Collect them all in a bowl or jar. Have one person randomly choose a name from the jar. That person is now the leader.

- **For a specific period of time, such as one class period or even an entire day, the leader makes all the rules for the entire group.** He or she decides how things are done, who does them, and who can and can't participate in activities. The only limitation, unlike in some totalitarian countries, is that the leader can't make anyone do anything that might be dangerous or harmful.

- **The leader should try to set some rules or create situations where other students are forced to do something they object to.** For example, all people with a certain hair or eye color have to clean the classroom, or people wearing a certain color of clothing can sit and have their lunches brought to them by other kids. Does this sound fair? Why or why not?

- **The next day, everyone evaluates the leader.** Discuss what it was like to be ruled by someone chosen randomly who wasn't obligated to follow certain rules or to be fair and equal, as a teacher or parent would have been. What if this person had been a bully or was really mean? What if this person only had his or her own interests in mind? What if your parents or your teacher did whatever this person wanted? How might this compare to living in a country ruled by a dictator or a totalitarian regime?

To investigate more, write a letter in protest of the leader's actions. Explain why you didn't like being ruled over by this person. Would this letter make a difference in a dictatorship? What about in a democracy?

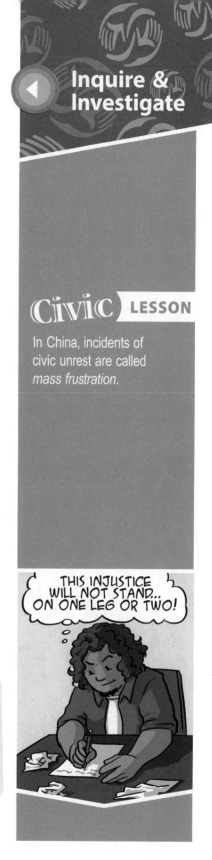

Civic LESSON

In China, incidents of civic unrest are called *mass frustration.*

HOW MANY PARTIES?

Imagine that the administration of your school has decided that it will no longer allow vending machines on campus. This is a topic that has caused controversy throughout the school. Students, teachers, and administrators fall on both sides of the issue. Looking at this kind of scenario can help you see the pros and cons of a two-party system.

- **Make a list of the different groups or factions that are involved in the issue.** Perhaps there is a group of students who feel it is their right to buy junk food. Another group might be worried about the loss of revenue from the vending machines, which has been

VOCAB LAB 📖

Write down what you think each word means: **freedom, monarchy, parliament, protest, totalitarian, dictator, ideology, communism, republic, persecute,** and **bill of rights**.

Compare your definitions with those of your friends or classmates. Did you all come up with the same meanings? Turn to the text and glossary if you need help.

used for school clubs. Think of as many groups as you can that would approach this issue with different concerns or agendas.

- **How many different factions did you come up with?** Do one or two factions seem to have a more popular perspective than the others? If you are working with fellow students or friends, vote on which two factions seem to best represent the viewpoint of most of the students.

- **Can you compare these factions to political parties?** Do you think the other factions, which aren't as popular, will have as much power to create change or persuade people? Why or why not?

- **Create one poster or flyer for each faction, and hang them on the walls of your classroom.** Have each person in the class vote for the poster that he or she thinks best represents his or her viewpoint. Which faction seems to be the most popular?

To investigate more, think of ways for the different factions to advertise their opinions about the vending machines. They might hang posters, hold a rally, or use social media. Do you think campaigning can change people's minds about an issue? Why or why not?

JUST FOR FUN

Here's a new twist on cootie catchers from the National Constitution Center! Print out the diagram and fold on the lines. Can you guess the rights hidden behind each of the first 10 amendments? How could you modify this cootie catcher to quiz your friends about other aspects of the Constitution?

HEYITSME   13M

28 LIKES
HEYITSME BRING BACK
THE VENDING MACHINES!
#SELFIESFORSNACKS

Chapter 2
Vive la Revolution!

Why do countries experience revolution?

Civic LESSON

"We then were ordered by our commander to open the hatches and take out all the chests of tea and throw them overboard, and we immediately proceeded to execute his orders, first cutting and splitting the chests with our tomahawks, so as thoroughly to expose them to the effects of the water. In about three hours . . . , we had thus broken and thrown overboard every tea chest to be found in the ship . . . . We were surrounded by British armed ships, but no attempt was made to resist us."

George Hewes, whose words are quoted above, was part of a gang of men dressed as Native Americans who dumped more than 92,000 pounds of tea into Boston Harbor during the night of December 16, 1773. The Boston Tea Party was an incident of civic unrest, one of many leading up to the American Revolution.

A revolution is a forcible overthrow of an existing government. It is a dangerous process that usually causes many deaths and disrupts the economic structures of the colony or country that's revolting.

Is a revolution worth it? Why do people revolt if they know they might lose their lives? Two critical reasons can often be found behind a people's incitement for change. One is a sense of injustice. This is the feeling that people are not being treated fairly by their government. The other is a lack of representation in their government, the impression that their voices are not being heard and that no one is looking out for their interests.

When citizens are no longer willing to live under conditions of injustice and lack of representation, they protest. Sometimes their protests lead to revolution.

> George Hewes and his fellow revolutionaries finally decided that the feelings of injustice outweighed the risk of protest.

POLITICAL INJUSTICE AND LACK OF REPRESENTATION

Have you ever experienced an injustice, either at school, at home, or while out with friends? Perhaps you have been unfairly punished for the behavior of a friend or sibling. It's never a pleasant experience.

Political injustice is what most often pushes people to take action against their government. This kind of injustice stems from situations, policies, or actions that impact and limit an individual's freedoms, such as free speech or the right to practice a chosen religion.

Civic LESSON

George Washington, who eventually led the colonial army and, later, the U.S. government, did not approve of the Boston Tea Party because it involved destruction of property.

The People Say

"...The inseparable twin of racial injustice was economic injustice."

—Martin Luther King Jr.,
American civil rights activist

MARTIN LUTHER KING JR.

Political injustice can also include policies or unfair procedures that limit the right to protection from cruel and unusual punishment. Remember Rosa Parks sitting on the city bus? How was the government limiting her freedom?

Lack of representation means people have no voice in their government. If people feel that nobody is defending their best interests or looking out for their welfare, it can destabilize a society. When a group of people, or even an entire country, feels as though it's invisible, that the needs and wants of individuals are not being addressed or considered, there is a lack of representation.

> Economic injustice is what people experience when they do not have the basic necessities of life, such as food and a safe place to live.

Economic injustice can also refer to the differences between those with great wealth and those who live in poverty. Large inequalities in wealth can create unequal opportunities for education, good jobs, and even proper healthcare.

People at the lower levels of income are at a disadvantage. They can begin to feel that they have not received their fair share of the benefits and resources that their government and society have to offer.

When citizens, or certain groups of citizens, feel that they are facing injustice from their government, they feel disempowered—that they have no ability to change their government. This is what leads to civic unrest, from petitions and peaceful protests all the way to actual violence. In the 1700s, American colonists were spurred by a sense of injustice to revolt against English rule and establish their own free nation.

THE AMERICAN REVOLUTION

Americans enjoy certain freedoms because they live in a democracy, but it wasn't always like that. Can you imagine living in the United States before it was the United States? Can you imagine having to pay taxes to a government you never agreed to?

America got its start when English explorers and settlers began colonies in places such as Jamestown and Plymouth. These people came in search of new resources for England or a place to escape religious persecution or to find new economic opportunities. In time, the 13 colonies found themselves increasingly dissatisfied with the way England ruled them. For one thing, England imposed very high taxes on the colonists. The Stamp Act and the Sugar Act taxed things that Americans used every day.

The Stamp Act, which taxed newspapers and a variety of documents, particularly angered Americans. Colonists wrote and signed petitions against the Stamp Act, refused to pay it, boycotted goods that required the tax, and even damaged property and harassed the officials charged with enforcing the act.

The perception of injustice and unfairness, and the lack of a true voice in the decisions directing the future of their countries, spur people to revolt.

After a great deal of work, the colonists did get Britain to repeal the tax. But it only served to emphasize the fact that Americans did not have representatives in the British government who were working specifically on their behalf.

The British continued to tax colonists with the Tea Act, which forced them to buy their tea only from the East India Company. This injustice pushed the colonists to the breaking point. That's when George Hewes, along with more than 100 other men, dumped more than 300 crates of tea into Boston Harbor in 1773.

The British responded by closing Boston Harbor and restricting the colonists' ability to meet in groups without the approval of the royal governor in Boston. The freedom we enjoy now, the freedom to assemble, had not yet been established. The colonists now had even less power to make their voices heard.

The colonists began meeting in secret. In 1774, delegates from almost every colony came together for the First Continental Congress. They met to discuss what to do about the growing trouble with the British.

Some colonies wanted war. Others felt that they were hopelessly outnumbered by the British soldiers, who were better trained.

> Throughout the war, colonists disagreed about how best to handle the strife, but on April 19, 1775, the first shots of the Revolutionary War were fired in Lexington, Massachusetts.

It was a long and bloody war for the colonists. But even as the British seemed to win most of the major battles, the revolutionaries persisted. In 1775, they held a Second Continental Congress and issued the Declaration of Independence the following year, in which they expressed all the injustices and offenses that Britain had committed against Americans.

By 1777, the tide of the war turned, and the Americans began to win. The British surrendered to George Washington in 1781, and in 1783 the Treaty of Paris officially declared peace. America—now the United States of America—had won its independence.

Like most revolutions, America's road to independence started with dissatisfaction with injustice. Americans rebelled against the injustices and lack of representation suffered by the colonists under British rule.

The results of the American Revolution didn't just affect Americans. Their successful war of independence also inspired other people to fight for changes in their governments.

POOR RICHARD'S ALMANACK

Benjamin Franklin wrote extensively about the colonies and their quest to be free. He often used a pseudonym for protection. One of these pseudonyms was Richard Saunders. You can view a digital copy of a 1914 collection of his quotes from *Poor Richard's Almanack*. Do you think Franklin would have used a pseudonym if he'd published after the Bill of Rights had been ratified? Do his quotes seem right for life today?

Just as the eighteenth century saw revolution spread across many countries, the twenty-first century watched Middle Eastern countries begin the hard journey toward democracy in a period known as the Arab Spring.

CiViC LESSON

The shortest revolution in American history was the Kemper Rebellion in 1810. Three brothers, Reuben, Nathan, and Samuel, declared West Florida to be independent from Spain, which controlled Florida at that time. The Republic of Florida lasted only 90 days before the United States annexed the territory.

THE FRENCH REVOLUTION

People on the other side of the Atlantic Ocean listened to news about the American Revolution with interest. Could a fight for freedom make a difference in how a country was ruled?

For most people who lived in Europe during the eighteenth century, life was one of poverty. A person's quality of life depended on the status that person was born with. No matter how hard you worked, you couldn't change your status.

If you were born to a wealthy family, you enjoyed comforts, pleasures, and recreation. But if you were similar to 97 percent of Europeans, you were born into a poor family, and poverty and hard work were all you ever knew. You struggled to survive, and there was nothing you could do to change that.

The people on the bottom level of society grew more and more resentful. In 1776, when Europeans heard about the British colonists in America rebelling against British rule, it gave them hope. If the Americans could fight against one of the more powerful military countries in the world, then perhaps the peasants of Europe could fight back against the wealthy aristocracy and create a new, fairer society.

> Once again, injustice and lack of representation were catalysts for change.

In France, the inequality between rich and poor was especially bad. French aristocrats were some of the richest people in the world. They owned huge pieces of land and controlled tremendous wealth and power.

> Because there was no parliament in France to control the power of the aristocrats and the king—as there was in Britain—the situation kept growing worse.

French society was divided into three groups, called estates. The highest estate consisted of priests and religious leaders. The second estate was made of the nobility, or the aristocrats. The third and lowest estate included everyone else, that 97 percent who were poor and barely surviving. They were miserable.

Peasants were forced to work on the land of the wealthy for very little pay. Plus they had to pay dues and rents to the aristocratic owners. They were mistreated and abused, and many were sick and starving. They had very few rights and no political power.

The members of the third estate in France rebelled. They formed the National Assembly to create a new constitution and impose reforms on the monarchy of King Louis XVI.

PIECE OF CAKE

One of the most famous stories of the French Revolution was of Marie Antoinette, the French queen, who, when told her subjects didn't have enough bread, supposedly said, "Let them eat cake." However, now historians don't believe that she actually said this. Thinking critically about anecdotes is part of being an effective historian.

New reforms resulted from the French Revolution, including abolishing the taxes imposed on peasants by their lords and requiring members of the first and second estates to pay taxes.

The People Say

"It was the best of times, it was the worst of times, it was the age of wisdom, it was the age of foolishness, it was the epoch of belief, it was the epoch of incredulity, it was the season of light, it was the season of darkness, it was the spring of hope, it was the winter of despair."

—Charles Dickens, English novelist, writing about the French Revolution

Fearful that the king would put an end to the National Assembly and its reforms, in 1789 the peasants attacked the Prison of Bastille and took weapons and ammunition.

> After a battle in which both rioters and soldiers were killed, the rioters took control of the prison and established a new, radical government. The French Revolution had begun.

News of the riots spread through the French countryside, and peasants began revolting against their aristocratic lords. This wave of violence was called the Great Fear, as peasants broke into manor houses to kill the nobles and steal from their estates.

Despite the violence raging in rural parts of the country, members of the first and second estates refused to give up their special privileges. They resisted granting equal rights to the members of the third estate.

Finally, after several weeks of rebellion, the third estate won and the National Assembly passed reforms that would improve the lives of the people living in poverty. They also created a bill of rights for the French people, which included freedom of speech, the press, and religion. These are still part of the French constitution.

REVOLTS IN LATIN AMERICA

Several revolutions have taken place in Latin America. These revolutions have often been born out of the same issues as the American and French revolutions—injustice and lack of representation.

From 1899 to 1902, Colombia was enmeshed in the Thousand Days' War. This conflict was a clash between the two ruling political parties. The Liberals wanted the individual states of Colombia to have more power, as well as reforms concerning peasants and land use. The Conservatives, however, wanted a strong central government. This party consisted mainly of the aristocracy, which didn't want to change the existing system.

In 1898 a new Colombian president was elected—conservative Manuel Antonio Sanclemente. Liberals believed his win was due to election fraud.

The new president was old and not very powerful, so the Liberals thought it was a good time to stage a rebellion. However, this particular revolution did not completely succeed. After 130,000 people died in a long and bloody war, the Liberals signed a cease-fire treaty with the Conservatives.

GLIMPSE OF HISTORY

Visit here to view photographs from the Mexican Revolution.

PITFALLS OF SELF-GOVERNING

Democracy is a high ideal that many countries strive for and often achieve. But what are the pitfalls of self-governing? One comes from the fact that officials are elected by popular vote. Not all citizens of a country will understand the political issues, and they might make the wrong choices in an election as a result. People might also be influenced by mobs or mass opinions, and neglect to use their own judgment because of the stronger opinions of those around them or in the media. And since officials are elected on a short-term basis, they may not have time to focus on forming a solid agenda. They could be more concerned about reelection than serving their people.

The Conservatives did institute some reforms, such as free elections and other economic and political reforms. But they didn't meet all of the demands of the Liberals.

The Mexican Revolution of 1910 was a transition from a dictatorship to a constitutional republic. Again, this conflict was sparked by people who felt that they had no power to express their opinions or choose who their public officials would be. And, just as in France, the wealth of the country was concentrated within a small group of people.

The president, Porfirio Díaz, had been in power for a long time. This was despite the fact that the Mexican Constitution called for public elections and other democratic processes.

[
A new group of young political leaders wanted to start participating in their country's government, but Díaz and his supporters blocked them.
]

The reformers, who wanted universal voting rights and a one-term limit on the presidency, called for Díaz to renounce his power. They elected their own temporary president to rule until new elections could be held.

The temporary president called for an uprising against the existing government, which sparked the Mexican Revolution in 1910. Revolts took place across the country as peasants rose up to claim their rights to local land and water, and revolt against Díaz and his followers. Díaz was ultimately defeated and a new president was elected in a national election.

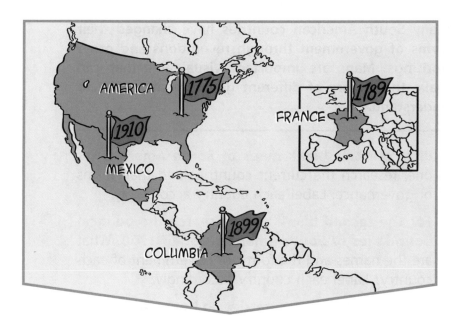

SING ME A REVOLUTION

A corrido is a song that celebrates a significant event or person in Mexican history. Click here to listen to a corrido that tells the tale of General Emiliano Zapata, who was one of the leaders of the Mexican Revolution.

Political injustice and lack of representation are the two most common reasons for revolution. But what happens after the revolution, when the revolutionaries have to turn their attention to governing the country they've created?

KEY QUESTIONS

- **How were the revolutions in America, France, and Latin America similar? How were they different?**

- **Would you have been a patriot or a loyalist in colonial America? Why?**

- **Are revolutions inevitable when a group of people is ruled over by another group?**

- **Are taxes necessary? What would the United States be like if there were no taxes?**

MAPPING IT

Many South American countries have changed their forms of government through revolutions and other uprisings. Maps are important visual aids that can make the history of different governments easier to understand.

- **Print out two blank maps of South America.** For one, research the current countries and their forms of governance. Label each country accordingly.

- **For the second blank map, research the political boundaries of South America around 1700.** What are the names and the forms of government of each country? Label each country accordingly.

- **Now, color code the countries on both maps, using a different color for each form of government.** What does this show you about shifts and patterns in governments? Is there a link or pattern to countries that are close to each other shifting to the same forms of government?

- **Study both maps and compare the differences.** How many of these countries have undergone a revolution between 1700 and today? Are there countries that started out as more democratic and are now closer to a different form of government?

> To investigate more, try the same exercise on the other continents. How does Africa or Asia compare to South America? Can you explain the similarities and differences?

THAT'S NOT FAIR . . . OR IS IT?

Not everyone who lived in the American colonies wanted independence from the British. Many colonists relied on British support for their livelihoods. Just as in America today, there were many different viewpoints in colonial America.

- **What if you were a patriot in the American colonies in the years before the American Revolution?** King George has already imposed the Stamp Act and the Sugar Act. As a patriot, write a letter to King George protesting his unfair policies and asking for Americans to have fair representation and treatment under the British rule.

- **Now, write a letter from the point of view of a supporter of British rule.** If you addressed your letter to a local Boston newspaper, how would you try to convince your fellow colonists that they should remain subjects of British leadership? What different arguments can you use to convince people? Do you try to appeal to their emotions or their sense of reason?

To investigate more, draw a political cartoon from the point of view of your choice. Does a cartoon have as much power as written text? Does humor make it harder or easier for you to convey an opinion about a political conflict?

JOIN OR DIE

Benjamin Franklin published a political cartoon in *The Pennsylvania Gazette* on May 9, 1754, showing several American colonies as parts of a snake cut into pieces. It is the earliest representation of colonial union. The cartoon became a symbol of colonial freedom during the American Revolutionary War.

JOIN, or DIE.

ON TRIAL

Imagine that you are part of the National Assembly during the French Revolution. You are involved in the 1793 trial proceedings of the revolutionary tribunal court against people who are accused of being part of the counterrevolutionary forces. These are people accused of working against the revolution.

- **Research Maximilien Robespierre and his role in the tribunal court.** Choose one student or group member to play Robespierre.

OFF WITH THEIR HEADS!

WE HEARD YOU THE *FIRST* TIME, ROBESPIERRE.

- **Research one of Robespierre's most famous cases, such as the court case against Marie Antoinette, or create your own case.** These could involve a supporter of the monarchy or a member of the aristocracy who is accused of working against the revolution. Or it could be for crimes against the peasants under their rule. Choose a student to play the role of defender and another to play the role of the defendant.

- **Choose six students to play the roles of jurors.** They are members of the third estate and are not aristocrats or religious leaders.

- **Hold a mock court proceeding.** Robespierre is the prosecutor, arguing against the defendant's legal representative.

- **The jury decides who has "won" the case.** It should base its decision on the history of the French Revolution. It will also decide what the punishment will be if the defendant is found guilty.

> To investigate more, consider that Robespierre was executed toward the end of the Reign of Terror. Why do you think the public's attitude toward him changed so drastically? Do you think his death showed that the revolutionaries were out of control or that they didn't fear demanding what they thought was right?

The People Say

"Today's the actual performance. You'll be surprised how well I know my role."
—**A French military officer on his way to the guillotine**

The guillotine became a gruesome symbol of the French Revolution as thousands of people were beheaded for being counterrevolutionary. It was important to many people that they remain calm right before their executions, so they would rehearse the moment of their deaths in preparation for the real thing.

Chapter 3

The Global Struggle for Democracy

How do other countries work toward democracy through civic unrest?

Many countries around the world are working toward a democratic government. People who struggle under communism, totalitarianism, or other strict regimes might use civic unrest to try and change their living conditions, increase the degree of freedom in their lives, and gain representation in government.

TIANANMEN SQUARE

On June 4, 1989, Chinese troops fired on thousands of civilians, including many students, who were protesting in Tiananmen Square. To this day, the Chinese military has not released the number of people who were killed and injured. Estimates range from a few hundred people to thousands of people.

The Tiananmen Square protest is an example of citizens practicing civic unrest with the goal of changing their government.

China is a communist country. Remember, communism is a form of rule in which the government owns all of the means of production. It owns all the factories, companies, and farms, as well as all the trucks, boats, trains, and other means of transportation. Freedom of the press and other freedoms that Americans take for granted are restricted. Many people in China feel the citizens should be free.

> Since 1949, when the Communist Party took over, people have staged protests, even though civic unrest is against the law.

The protests in Tiananmen Square were sparked by the death of a former Communist party leader, Hu Yaobang, in April 1989. Yaobang had worked to move China toward a more open form of government, and he had become a symbol of a democratic reform movement. When he died, thousands of Chinese students marched though the capital city of Beijing to Tiananmen Square.

The protests lasted for weeks. One of the most famous images to come from any protest movement is that of a single man, known as Tank Man, standing in front of tanks in a street in Beijing. He stood there blocking the tanks on June 5, 1989, the day after the protesters in Tiananmen Square were fired upon by Chinese troops.

As a column of Chinese tanks moved toward him down the otherwise deserted street, he stood calmly, blocking its way. The tanks came to a halt, and then the lead tank tried to steer around the young man. He kept stepping into its path. The young man, who is still known only as Tank Man, held his ground until he was taken away. No one knows what happened to him afterward, but the photograph of this man in front of the tanks quickly made its way around the world.

THE HAMMER AND SICKLE ARE SYMBOLS OF THE COMMUNIST PARTY.

The Tiananmen Square protests did not result in any lasting changes in the Chinese government. However, it was an extremely important event because it showed that even citizens ruled by a communist government can still make their voices heard. These people have many restrictions on their personal lives but they still gathered together with the hope of accomplishing change in their country.

THE ARAB SPRING

What do people who live in countries where there are no elections do? Sometimes, they resort to rebellion to gain the right to political representation.

Remember how the American Revolution influenced the French Revolution? This is exactly what happened during a period of time known as the Arab Spring. One group's bravery in one country empowered others to make their voices heard.

The first protests occurred in Tunisia in December 2010. During the following months, what came to be known as the Arab Spring spread across the Middle East and North Africa. Some of the protests were aimed at local governments and were sparked by humanitarian issues. These included the imbalance of wealth between rich and poor, government corruption, increasing food prices, and famine.

There was also a growing class of people who had become better educated and were seeking a higher standard of living. They wanted governments that were willing to make reforms.

The protests shared some aspects of civic unrest used in other countries, such as strikes, demonstrations, and rallies. But these tactics were often met with violence from the government and military, as well as from counterprotesters.

The uprisings that began in Tunisia spread to Egypt, Libya, and Yemen, where government rulers were forced out of power. In other places, such as Bahrain and Syria, more civic uprisings occurred, and both major and minor protests took place in Algeria, Iraq, Jordan, Kuwait, Morocco, Saudi Arabia, Sudan, and the Palestinian Territories.

> The slogan of many of the Arab Spring protesters was "the people want to bring down the regime."

Many of the protests led to elections in those countries. Tunisia held national elections for the first time since 1956. In Egypt, elections were considered to be far more fair than they had been under the regime of President Hosni Mubarak, who ruled for almost 30 years by using fraud and intimidation at the polls.

We don't know what the lasting changes from the Arab Spring will be, but it's exciting to see citizens demand the change they know their country needs.

The People Say

"The people want to bring down the regime."
—**Arab Spring slogan**

The Arab Spring protests were some of the first to use social media, blogs, and websites to raise awareness and to organize and communicate.

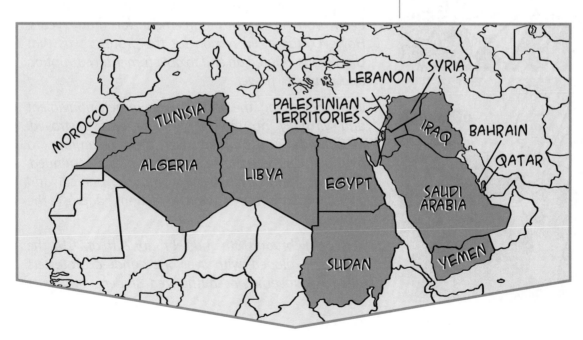

A VOICE FROM UKRAINE, 2014

Civic unrest in Ukraine beginning in late 2013 made daily headlines around the world. The political disruption in Ukraine illustrated some of the possible reasons for civic unrest—and the potential outcomes of protest and dissent.

J. Tedrowe Bonner, an American sociologist, was in Ukraine during this time and wrote about the protests in Kiev.

In November of 2013, the "Euromaidan" protests began in Kiev, the capital of Ukraine. Over four months, as many as a million people showed up from different parts of Ukraine to protest, with thousands of people setting up camps right in the middle of Maidan Nezalezhnosti (Independence Square), where the government buildings are located. Citizens from all over the country literally moved in to the heart of the city.

The reason the protests started was because President Viktor Yanukovych refused to sign a free trade agreement with the European Union. Ukraine had been working on this agreement for many years. However, the main reason for the protests was that Ukrainians wanted an end to governmental corruption and abuse of power.

In the beginning, the protests were largely nonviolent and virtually no private property was destroyed. McDonald's even turned over their restaurant to help people. Nevertheless, as the protests continued, President Yanukovych became more tyrannical and eventually authorized violent actions against the protesters.

Between February 18th and February 20th of 2014, the violence exploded, with over one hundred protesters killed by government authorized snipers, and over

VIKTOR YANUKOVYCH

one thousand people injured. In addition, a handful of police officers were killed. By February 22nd Victor Yanukovych vacated his position as president while the Ukrainian parliament simultaneously voted to impeach him.

> As one Ukrainian noted, "It is the point between the past and the future. It is a very good lesson."

However, in the wake of the Euromaidan protests, a backlash has occurred in the eastern part of Ukraine, where small groups of illegally armed men have taken over government buildings in certain regions. Their argument is that if protesters in Kiev had the right to overthrow the central government, they should have the right to overthrow the regional government. These people see President Yanukovych's removal as an illegal overthrow of a legitimate government, and are seeking to create their own nation.

How do we determine when social unrest represents the will of the people? Is violence ever healthy in social unrest? If so, what forms of violence seem helpful? Do regions of a country have the right to separate, even when it is the will of the people?

Euromaidan has captured the imagination of the world since in many countries people are fighting again corrupt, abusive governments.

—J. Tedrowe Bonner, April 2014

 The People Say

"It was not about Europe anymore, but about stopping the violence against peaceful protesters, ensuring justice, and demanding the resignation of the criminal government and its president."

—**Anastasiia, Euromaidan protester**

KEY QUESTIONS

- **Why were people protesting in Tiananmen Square in 1989?**
- **How was this protest different from the protests of Arab Spring? How was it similar?**

LET'S COMPARE

What would it be like to live in China? Would it be much different from how you live now?

One of the best ways to see the differences between types of governments is to compare what they have in common and what's different.

- **Research the characteristics of the United States government and the government of Communist China.** Make a list for each government that addresses topics such as human rights, elections, and freedoms. Add topics such as being able to travel easily or the freedom to speak out against political figures.

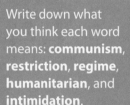

VOCAB LAB

Write down what you think each word means: **communism**, **restriction**, **regime**, **humanitarian**, and **intimidation**.

Compare your definitions with those of your friends or classmates. Did you all come up with the same meanings? Turn to the text and glossary if you need help.

- **Make a Venn diagram that compares these two governments.** Created by John Venn in 1880, Venn diagrams are used to discover relationships between different groups. Your Venn diagram should intersect where China and the United States have government characteristics in common.

- **What can you tell from looking at the completed diagram?** Do these governments have more things in common or more things that are different?

To investigate more, create Venn diagrams to illustrate the differences and similarities between the United States and another country, such as South Africa or Haiti. Are you surprised by any of your comparisons?

Inquire & Investigate

Print a world map as large as you want at this website.

SO...WHAT COLOR SHOULD WE MAKE ANTARCTICA?

WHAT COLOR IS YOUR COUNTRY?

How many democracies are there in the world? How many monarchies? How many dictatorships?

- **Divide into three groups.** Each group will take a specific form of government—democracy, monarchy, or dictatorship/totalitarian regime. Find all the countries in the world that have that form of government. A good research source is the CIA World Factbook.

- **Assign each group its own color crayon or marker.** Find or print a large world map that shows all the countries, clearly defined. Each group colors in, with its particular color, all the countries in the world that use its form of government. If a group finds that there are countries that use a form of its government but with some variations, it can use a variation of its color to show that difference.

- **How does the finished map look?** Compare the number of countries of each color. What form of government has the most countries? The fewest? Are there blank countries? Why don't they fit?

To investigate more, choose a point in the past, such as during WWI or WWII, and complete this activity according to the types of government that were ruling countries at that time. If a country has been taken over by another country, it must be the same color as the conquering country. How is your historical map different from your current map? Can you spot any trends?

Chapter 4 ▶
Civil Rights in America

Why is it important that everyone has equal rights and is treated fairly?

When Rosa Parks refused to give up her seat on the bus, she was taking part in a rich tradition of protest. Long before the Civil Rights movement of the 1960s, workers and women fought for equal rights using the same methods of marching, demonstrating, striking, and uniting individuals into more powerful groups. Throughout American history, many civil rights issues have been fought over by people who saw a need for change and decided to be a part of the solution.

Today, people in the United States are still standing up for the principles and ideals they believe in. What issues do you feel strongly about?

> Civic unrest usually occurs when citizens feel that their civil rights are being violated.

WORKERS' RIGHTS

The fight for workers' rights in the United States is almost as old as the country itself. This struggle was born from the need to protect workers from unsafe working conditions and unfair practices.

Workers have fought for reasonable working hours. They have worked for health insurance and compensation in case they were injured or sick. Protesters also fought to end child labor.

Workers have struggled for their rights using two methods. During strikes and protests, they refused to work and often marched in the streets to gain publicity for their cause. Workers have also organized labor unions. These are common interest groups formed around particular industries. They serve as a way to unite workers together in order to be more powerful.

> The earliest recorded strike in the United States took place in 1768, when tailors went on strike in New York to protest a cut in pay.

The first labor union was formed in Philadelphia in 1794, when shoemakers came together to form a group. In the 1800s, many trade unions grew to include workers in many states instead of just in single cities, and they became better organized in the process.

Unions enabled their members to benefit from collective bargaining, which is when workers bargain with employers for better working conditions or higher pay. Workers who are organized together in a union can use the power of their large number of members and the threat of strike to stand up for their rights.

Some groups of workers were not represented by the early labor unions. Women, immigrants, and African Americans had to form their own unions. Young women

The People Say

"With all their faults, trade-unions have done more for humanity than any other organization of men that ever existed. They have done more for decency, for honesty, for education, for the betterment of the race, for the developing of character in man, than any other association of men."

—Clarence Darrow, American lawyer and member of the American Civil Liberties Union

Civic LESSON

Strikes could sometimes backfire and escalate into violence. In 1877, coal miners went on strike in Pennsylvania and many died in the violence between striking workers and armed militia. In 1914, another strike by coal miners in Colorado resulted in the deaths of 13 women and children and nine men.

THE TRIANGLE FIRE

Listen to the voices of female workers from the Triangle Shirtwaist Factory who escaped the fire that killed nearly 150 people.

working in the textile mills of Lowell, Massachusetts, were moved to "turn out" as a group to protest wage cuts in 1834. In 1843, they formed the Lowell Female Labor Reform Association and began public petitions for a 10-hour workday.

In 1909, 20,000 women working in the garment trade in New York went on strike to protest the sweatshop conditions they worked in. Sadly, this was followed two years later by the deaths of 150 women in the Triangle Shirtwaist Factory fire.

> Workers in the Triangle Shirtwaist Factory fire died because there weren't enough exits and because factory managers had kept some of the doors locked to prevent theft.

African Americans also struggled to find representation in labor unions. Movements such as the Pullman boycott in 1894 led to a general railroad workers strike. The creation of the Brotherhood of Sleeping Car Porters in 1925 helped create labor support for African Americans.

Powerful business owners did their best to prevent workers from protesting or striking for higher pay and better treatment. Improved working conditions cost money. Higher wages mean higher prices. But the Constitution grants people the right to gather together and voice their opinions. By the end of World War II, more than 12 million workers belonged to labor unions.

Through the decades, labor unions have made it possible for a stronger labor force that enjoys reasonable workdays, better pay, and more humane working conditions.

CIVIC LESSON

Every year at the beginning of September, Americans observe Labor Day in honor of the long history of laborers. This holiday was first celebrated in 1882 with a march of about 10,000 people in New York City.

WOMEN'S RIGHTS

Do you think women are treated the same as men? Do they make as much money for the same work? Look at the people seated in Congress and the House of Representatives. What about the people in charge of large corporations? How many of them are women?

Another area of civil rights that owes its accomplishments to a great deal of civic unrest is women's rights. At the first women's rights convention, held in Seneca Falls, New York, in 1848, Elizabeth Cady Stanton drafted a declaration of sentiments and grievances that echoed the Declaration of Independence:

"We hold these truths to be self-evident: that all men and women are created equal."

From the start, women working for equal rights demanded the rights that were written in the Constitution but seemed to have been limited to men. At the same time, women used the rights of peaceful assembly and freedom of speech and the press to advance their cause.

At first, the women's rights movement focused on correcting the things that limited women's abilities to succeed. These included lack of educational opportunities and too many family responsibilities. Women had few economic opportunities of their own and sought a voice in politics. Eventually, much of the women's movement focused on suffrage, or the right of women to vote in American elections.

WHERE ARE THE WOMEN?

In 2014, 79 of the 435 members of the House of Representatives consisted of women. That's just more than 18 percent. Only 4.8 percent of the world's most profitable businesses were led by women. In 2012, women earned, on average, 9 percent less than men performing the same job.

SUFFERING FOR SUFFRAGE

Can you imagine a time when women were not allowed to vote? Today, that idea seems strange, but women had to fight for suffrage and for equal rights.

They did this in many different ways. They put on parades where they marched with signs. They held pageants and gave speeches in the street. They picketed outside places where political leaders were giving speeches. They lobbied government officials and collected signatures on petitions.

All of these efforts brought them national attention. Eventually, women were able to gain enough political support for the passage in 1920 of the 19th Amendment to the Constitution, which guarantees women in America the right to vote.

One of the most famous names in the women's suffrage movement is Alice Paul. She was active in organizing parades and other events to publicize suffrage. She even met with President Woodrow Wilson about her cause.

Civic LESSON

The first state to grant women the right to vote was Wyoming Territory. It granted women suffrage in 1869, 51 years before the 19th Amendment.

When parades and lobbying Congress didn't work, Paul organized 18 months of picketing in front of the White House, starting in January 1917. These women were often attacked and abused. Many of them, including Alice Paul, were sent to jail.

> More than 1,000 women, called "Silent Sentinels," marched slowly day and night, holding banners with slogans such as "Mr. President, how long must women wait for liberty?"

They went on hunger strikes in jail and performed acts of civil disobedience. This is a peaceful form of protest during which they refused to follow rules but did not fight back or use violence. They were often force fed, which meant food was put in their stomachs through tubes inserted down their throats. Sometimes, the women were sent to insane asylums. But by 1918, President Wilson publicly supported suffrage, and in 1920, the work of Alice Paul and many others resulted in the 19th Amendment to the Constitution.

ALL MEN ARE CREATED EQUAL?

Another important example of the fight for civil rights in action is the Civil Rights movement of the 1960s. It was a long struggle for African Americans to gain equal rights as American citizens and to fight against racial segregation and prejudice.

Civic LESSON

The responsibility of every U.S. citizen is to practice civic engagement. This means not only being educated about their government, but also actively participating to make a difference in their communities and country. A citizen practicing civic engagement, which may include participating in civic unrest, recognizes that every problem in their community or government is also their problem, and that it is important to make informed and intelligent decisions and take action when necessary.

Martin Luther King Jr. wrote the following in a letter in 1963 detailing his reasons for civic unrest.

"But when you have seen vicious mobs lynch your mothers and fathers at will and drown your sisters and brothers at whim . . . when you suddenly find your tongue twisted and your speech stammering as you seek to explain to your six year old daughter why she can't go to the public amusement park that has just been advertised on television, and see tears welling up in her eyes when she is told that Funtown is closed to colored children... when you have to concoct an answer for a five year old son who is asking: 'Daddy, why do white people treat colored people so mean?' . . . then you will understand why we find it difficult to wait."

PS

In the 1960s, particularly in the Southern states, African Americans were treated as inferior to whites in almost every aspect of society. They were segregated in schools, on public transportation, in restaurants, and on the job. Many communities passed rules that made it difficult for African Americans to vote. The Civil Rights movement attempted to correct these inequalities, end segregation, and restore the right to vote to every U.S. citizen, regardless of race.

> One of America's most famous civil rights activists, who followed the principles of civil disobedience and nonviolent protest, was Martin Luther King Jr.

Martin Luther King Jr. was always an active participant in the Civil Rights movement to bring equal rights to African Americans, and eventually he became the movement's most famous leader. He made speeches, wrote books, and organized and participated in peace marches, demonstrations, boycotts, and voter registration drives. He received frequent death threats and his home was bombed. He was arrested at least 20 times and he was assaulted frequently. Martin Luther King Jr. also received the Nobel Peace Prize in 1964. He is still revered for his role in advancing civil rights.

Many people involved in the Civil Rights movement engaged in civil disobedience. They went to sit-ins, during which they occupied lunch counters, the front seats of buses, and any other areas that were supposedly for whites only. They simply refused to leave, then passively allowed themselves to be removed by police.

Supporters of the Civil Rights movement organized voter registration drives to make it possible for all people to register to vote. They also used boycotts, demonstrations, marches, mass media, and lawsuits to advance their cause.

Even children participated in civic unrest and protests. The most famous is the Birmingham Children's March, called the Children's Crusade. On May 2, 1963, thousands of black children in Birmingham, Alabama, skipped school and marched downtown in protest. Hundreds were arrested, but more marched the next day.

The children were crowded into jail cells without enough food, water, or sanitation. During the marches, some children were blasted with high-power fire hoses, hit by police, and attacked by police dogs. But the children continued to march, and images of their marches and their treatment by officials were broadcast around the world. Through their actions, these brave children gained support for the Civil Rights movement.

The Civil Rights movement grew so large and disruptive, and spawned enough incidents of violence against both black and white civil rights participants, that the federal government had to step in. New laws overturned segregation laws and restored voting rights. The laws made it illegal to discriminate against African Americans in housing, education, or employment.

THE BATTLE OF SEATTLE

You might think that the fight for civil rights lies in the past, but instances of civic unrest for the sake of making conditions more fair to everyone happen every day.

WE SHALL OVERCOME

Protest songs are valuable tools in protest movements. During the Civil Rights movement, the song "We Shall Overcome" became a symbol of the dream of equal rights.

"We Shall Overcome" came from a song sung by slaves during the Civil War:

"I'll be all right someday I'll overcome someday."

The song was adopted in places as far away as China, Korea, South Africa, and Lebanon during protest movements there.

Listen to folk singer Pete Seeger sing "We Shall Overcome." Why do you think the song was inspiring to so many people working for civil rights? Can you think of songs sung today that have the same uniting effect?

Seattle isn't the only place to have seen protests against the power of large corporations over poor countries. Many cities, including Hong Kong, Geneva, New Delhi, and Bali have seen hundreds and thousands of people march in support of fair and sustainable global trade.

FREEDOM OF THE PRESS

Television, print media, and radio covered the protests in Seattle. Through these news programs, the world could see exactly what was happening and hear the voices of the protesters themselves. Why was it important for the public to know what the protesters were doing and how law enforcement handled it?

[In 1999, between 50,000 and 100,000 people protested in the rainy streets of Seattle, Washington, not against a government but against an idea: globalization.]

These protesters were marching for fair trade and labor rights, which they felt the World Trade Organization (WTO) didn't support. The WTO, founded in 1995, is an organization that regulates trade between its member countries all over the world. It provides a structure for countries to negotiate trade agreements and settle disputes between its 159 member countries.

The WTO was engaged in negotiating new trade agreements in Seattle when the massive protests took place. The protesters came from several different organizations, most of which were part of the anti-globalization movement.

Some of those protesters were nongovernment organizations (NGOs) involved with issues such as labor, the environment, and consumer protection. There were also student groups, religious groups, trade unions, and environmentalists.

Protesters blocked intersections, A few people resorted to looting and violence. Police used teargas and pepper spray to disperse the protesters, and eventually the National Guard was called in to restore order. The media came under fire for misreporting that the protesters were more violent than they really were.

The Battle of Seattle brought globalization to the attention of citizens and the media. The protests were successful for bringing the issue to the attention of a broader audience, rather than accomplishing a specific change.

THE TEA PARTY MOVEMENT

The Tea Party movement in the United States grew out of the unhappiness of many citizens with the way the government operates. It gets its name from the Boston Tea Party that preceded the American Revolution, when patriots protested against the British government.

Today's Tea Party wants to reduce the spending of the American government, and its level of debt and taxation. It wants to return to what it believes are the basic ideals of the U.S. Constitution and the Founding Fathers.

> The Tea Party has sparked renewed debate about the Constitution. Members of the Tea Party strongly believe that the constitution is the highest authority and should be upheld and protected.

Since 2009, the Tea Party has sponsored protests and supported political candidates from conservative and libertarian groups. It focuses on government reforms and has been linked with very conservative issues such as gun control, illegal immigration, and prayer in schools.

The People Say

"The original American patriots were those individuals brave enough to resist with force the oppressive power of King George.... Patriotism is more closely linked to dissent than it is to conformity and a blind desire for safety and security."

—**Ron Paul,**
Tea Party politician

Civic LESSON

During the first protest of the Tea Party on January 24, 2009, several of the protesters wore Native American headdresses. The patriots who participated in the Boston Tea Party in 1773 dressed as Native Americans when they dumped tea into Boston Harbor. Why did the protesters want to make that connection?

While the Tea Party has succeeded in getting many of its candidates into government, it is no longer seen as a movement so much as a new version or new side of the Republican political party. But it is a good example of ordinary Americans making their voices heard about their government, and acting in a way to get that message out and influence elections and issues.

WE ARE THE 99%

The U.S. Constitution assigns American citizens the responsibility to speak out against policies in their government they do not like. People can also protest against corporations, institutions, ideals—anything they believe does not fully benefit the people.

The Occupy Wall Street (OWS) movement started as a protest against greed and corruption. It organized against the strong influence of large corporations on the U.S. government and the growing inequality between the rich and the poor.

> How does this relate to the anti-globalization movement, which feels that huge international corporations seek maximum profits at the expense of fair labor practices, safe working conditions, and fair hiring and wage practices?

OWS adopted the slogan "We are the 99%." The OWS slogan is in reference to the fact that just 1 percent of Americans own more than a third of the wealth in the country. This leaves the remaining two-thirds to spread among 99 percent of the population.

The OWS movement was operated by consensus. This means that participants voted on what actions to take in a rare form of pure democracy.

The protesters marched and picketed and set up a protest camp in the financial district of New York City. They also used social media to advance their cause. After nearly two months of camping and demonstrating in Zuccotti Park, the protesters were forced to leave on November 15, 2011.

Protesters have occupied many other locations, including corporate headquarters, banks, college offices, and university quads. The OWS movement has been supported by labor unions and even some politicians, who feel that the protesters have the right to complain about the Americans responsible for creating many of the country's financial problems. Can these people be trusted to fix the problems they created?

The U.S. Constitution grants the right to people to protest practices they feel are unfair. The Civil Rights movement, the labor movement, and the women's rights movement are all examples of groups that have used this right to change the world.

OCCUPY WALL STREET

"America needs its own Tahrir" was the rallying cry of the Occupy Wall Street movement. The slogan refers to Tahrir Square in Egypt, which Arab Spring protesters had occupied in 2011, an occupation that eventually forced the resignation of Egyptian President Mubarak. Tahrir had become the focus of the demonstrations and a symbol of the movement for a change in government. With Tahrir in mind, the Canadian, anti-consumerism, pro-environmental magazine *Adbusters* called for an occupation of Zuccotti Park in New York City, near the Wall Street financial district, on September 17, 2011.

KEY QUESTIONS

- How is the fight for civil rights today different from the fight for civil rights in the past?

- Do all civil rights movements need a strong leader? Why or why not?

- What are some reasons behind discrimination? Why are women sometimes treated differently than men? Why are African Americans sometimes treated differently?

IT'S MY RIGHT

Even students have the power to change their government, or to protest when they think that their constitutional rights have been violated.

- **Research the Supreme Court case of Tinker v. Des Moines.** Students were able to prove in court that their constitutional rights were violated when they were not allowed to wear black armbands in school to protest the Vietnam War.

- **Imagine that you and a small group of friends have decided to protest a school policy.** For example, what if you wanted to protest against a policy that does not allow same-sex couples to attend the prom together. You are wearing rainbow ribbons and asking other students to sign a petition supporting your protest. The school's administration threatens to suspend you if you don't stop your protest.

- **Write a letter to the school board in which you present your case.** You are arguing why it is within your constitutional rights to protest against the school policy. Can you find and cite section(s) of the Constitution that pertain to your case? Can you find examples of other well-known court cases with similar situations?

- **Now imagine that the school board has called you into a meeting to present your case.** Write a statement or speech to read in order to convince them to change the policy.

> **To investigate more, think of other ways you can protest the school's policy. What can you do to present your objections in a meaningful and noticeable way?**

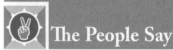

The People Say

"But I'm not concerned about that now. I just want to do God's will. And He's allowed me to go up to the mountain. And I've looked over. And I've seen the promised land. I may not get there with you. But I want you to know tonight, that we, as a people, will get to the promised land! . . ."

—**Martin Luther King Jr.**

In his last speech, given the night before he was assassinated in Memphis, Tennessee, on April 4, 1968. Martin Luther King Jr. was standing on the second floor balcony of a motel when he was shot.

PS

POLLS

During election season, your household may receive phone calls from people who want to conduct an opinion poll. They want to know who or what issues you'll be voting for in an upcoming election. Polls are a way for candidates and parties to gauge where they are in terms of voter popularity. It helps them get a feel for where they should stand on issues of importance to the voters. There are also exit polls, conducted by network television, that are aimed at voters who are leaving a voting place. By asking them who they voted for, the network can often get a feel for who might be winning an election. Exit polls are controversial, though. What negative effect do you think exit polls could have on the outcome of an election?

THE POLLS SAID . . .

Polls are important tools for political campaigns, but they're not always good predictors of election results. The Bradley effect is the controversial idea that white voters say they support an African American candidate during polling because they are embarrassed to admit that they wouldn't vote for a black person. Then, in the privacy of an election booth, they vote for the white candidate. The Bradley effect was named after Los Angeles Mayor Tom Bradley, an African-American who was ahead in voter polls in the 1982 governor's race in California but lost the election. Do a little research and see if you think this is a real phenomenon or not.

- **Research alleged instances of the Bradley effect, which is sometimes called the Wilder effect, online.** Gather information about the candidates. What did the polls predict the results of the elections would be?

- **Compare the polling results to the actual election results.** Which candidate was polling as the winner? Which candidate actually won the election?

- **Read articles and editorials about the possibility of the Bradley effect in that particular election.** Do you believe racism was a factor? Why or why not?

> To investigate more, read about the 1982 California governor's race, during which the Bradley effect was first hypothesized. What other factors could have contributed to the outcome of that race? What are some of the ways we could prevent bias in elections?

Chapter 5

Human Rights Around the World

What are human rights and how are they supported by civic unrest?

Human rights is the topic that civic unrest most often addresses. It is the idea that all human beings, no matter who they are or where they are, have certain basic rights. These include the right to life, freedom from torture, and freedom from slavery.

It's one thing to fight for civil rights within a democracy such as America. Our country grants its citizens the right to assemble and to speak and write freely. But there are places in the world where people have fought for civil rights in far less supportive conditions and still succeeded in their mission.

Sometimes, activists face great danger to themselves and their families when they stand up for what they believe is right. They might lose their jobs, receive threats and warnings, suffer imprisonment, and even risk their lives.

For many people, this only strengthens their resolve to fight for the ideals they believe in. Their rights are so trampled and the stakes are so high that they risk everything in their quest. It's because of people such as this that the world keeps improving and equality remains an achievable concept.

CIVIL RIGHTS AND SOUTH AFRICA

In 1948, the National Party gained power in South Africa. For 46 years under this government, until a new constitution was put into place in 1994, South Africa suffered under a policy of racial segregation known as apartheid.

Under apartheid, South Africans who were not white were forced to live in separate areas from whites and to use separate public facilities. They were only allowed to have limited contact with white people. This system violated the civil rights of a majority of South Africa's population and was opposed by many people both inside and outside of the country. Yet its laws remained in effect for almost 50 years.

South Africans showed resistance to the system through many forms: nonviolent protests, strikes, political action, demonstrations, and, eventually, armed resistance.

> During one mass meeting in 1952, attendees burned their pass books, which were the documents blacks were forced to carry to show that they were authorized to be in certain areas.

At another meeting, the people adopted a Freedom Charter that stated, "South Africa belongs to all who live in it, black or white." At this meeting, 150 people were arrested and charged with treason.

 The People Say

"To deny people their human rights is to challenge their very humanity."

—**Nelson Mandela, South African human rights leader**

NELSON MANDELA

MIRIAM MAKEBA

In 1960, protesters arrived at a police station intending to be arrested as a show of resistance, but at least 67 were killed and almost 200 injured. Many resistance leaders, including Nelson Mandela, were imprisoned. Mandela was jailed from 1963 until 1990, but his imprisonment drew international attention and helped create wide support for the anti-apartheid movement.

One of the most powerful protest tools of the apartheid era was music. It started in Africa, where African singers such as Miriam Makeba, Hugh Masekela, Youssou N'Dour, and the Malopoets used songs to protest against apartheid policies.

> As the movement grew and people in other parts of the world joined in, bands and singers—including U2, Bruce Springsteen, and Stevie Wonder—used songs to show their support for the anti-apartheid movement and for Nelson Mandela.

In 1985, guitarist Steven Van Zandt of Bruce Springsteen's E Street Band organized a boycott of Sun City. This resort town in South Africa always paid for big-name international singers to appear there. Van Zandt and several other artists, including Springsteen, U2's Bono, Miles Davis, and Run-DMC, wrote and recorded the song "I Ain't Gonna Play Sun City." The song brought the apartheid issue to a global audience.

South Africa gained even more international attention in 1976, when police opened fire on a crowd of children. The young people were protesting in Soweto, a South African township.

PROTEST BOOGIE

Different types of music have played powerful parts in civic unrest. Listen to Miriam Makeba sing a solemn song about a South African jail and different rock artists collaborate on a more rambunctious song. What roles does each type of music have to play in civic unrest? Which, if either, is more effective? Which evokes a response in you?

"Nongqongqo" by Miriam Makeba

"I Ain't Gonna Play Sun City" by various artists.

The widespread protests that followed, combined with an economic recession that affected the entire country, made it clear that apartheid was bad for South Africa. The United Nations, the United Kingdom, and the United States began imposing economic and military sanctions on South Africa. Slowly, over the years, some reforms were instituted.

Nelson Mandela was released from prison in 1990, despite the fact that he was serving a life sentence for sabotage against the apartheid government. By 1994, new elections and a new constitution marked an official end to apartheid. In what would have been an unthinkable turn of events just a few years before, Mandela became South Africa's first democratically elected president.

Civic unrest in South Africa was practiced through both nonviolent and violent means. It created change in a system that for many, many years seemed completely unchangeable.

 The People Say

"I have fought against white domination, and I have fought against black domination. I have cherished the ideal of a democratic and free society in which all persons live together in harmony and with equal opportunities. It is an ideal which I hope to live for and to achieve. But if needs be, it is an ideal for which I am prepared to die."

—Nelson Mandela, at the opening of his trial in 1964

 You can read Mandela's entire statement here.

BRITISH AND INDIAN

Life for the British living in India was often very comfortable, while life for Indians, most of whom lived in poverty, was difficult and dangerous. Look at these photos of life during the British Raj. What are some differences between the British experience and the Indian experience? What can you deduce from these photographs?

Civic LESSON

Many different languages are spoken in India. The main ones are Hindi, Bengali, Telugu, Marathi, Tamil, and Urdu. Do you think having many languages increases a country's sense of unity?

British rule over India began as early as the seventeenth century, when the British East India Company gained the right to set up trading posts along the coast of India. These trading posts eventually grew into major cities, including Madras, Bombay, and Calcutta.

As Britain defended its business centers from both the local population and the French, who wanted to establish its own trading in India, it gained more control over the country. Because Britain was so far away, it was easy for British East Indies Company leaders to fall into habits of corruption, such as taking bribes from powerful locals.

Racial tensions contributed to the unrest among Indians. Some British officials felt that native Indians were equal to white people, but more felt that European culture was superior to Indian culture.

Indian soldiers rebelled in the Great India Mutiny in 1857. The rebellion was sparked by the Indian troops rejecting the kind of grease they believed the British were using in rifles. Rumors of pig and cow fat used in rifles, which was forbidden by the Muslim and Hindu religions of the Indian people, illustrated the cultural insensitivity of the British. As a result of the Great India Mutiny the British government took over the rule of India from the British East India Company.

Britain ruled India from then until 1947, a period called the Raj. Many people in the lower classes were not treated well by the British businesses. Indian society was strictly divided into different castes, or groups.

Only people in the upper castes were able to work in high-paying jobs. Members of the lower castes, especially one called the untouchables, lived permanently in poverty with no possibility that their lives could be better.

The Indian National Congress, founded in 1885, led the independence movement. Native Indians, tired of being treated like second-class citizens, pushed to rule their own country according to their own traditions and beliefs. They participated in demonstrations, marches, and fasting. To challenge the oppressive British salt tax, the Indian people even made their own salt by boiling sea water.

THE UNTOUCHABLE CASTE

> The two main cultures in India, the Muslims and the Hindus, clashed over how the country would be governed. Many Muslims feared being a minority in a Hindu-ruled country, and wanted a new, separate state created for Muslims.

That's why, when India gained independence from Britain in 1947, Pakistan was founded in the north, as a separate country. This was the area where there was a Muslim majority.

India and Pakistan have had several conflicts since 1947. Tensions between the two countries remain high, even during peacetime. The strained relationship between India and Pakistan presents one of the most complicated diplomatic problems of today's world.

Civic LESSON

Mahatma Gandhi was a champion of nonviolent civic unrest who changed the world and influenced many others struggling for freedom and civil rights. He used the principles of civil disobedience to achieve independence for India from Great Britain.

The People Say

"Live as if you were to die tomorrow. Learn as if you were to live forever."

—**Mahatma Gandhi**

MAHATMA GANDHI

Civic LESSON

When South Africa's Nelson Mandela was awarded the Nobel Peace Prize in 1993, he donated his prize money to charity.

GANDHI'S LEGACY

Mahatma Gandhi was born and raised as a Hindu and attended law school in England. He led other Indians in protests and occupations, all done according to nonviolent civic unrest tactics. His goal for India was to achieve self-rule as a country, free from colonization by England.

> Gandhi was concerned about all people in Indian society. He worked toward strengthening women's rights, eliminating poverty, and building cooperation between different religious and ethnic groups.

Gandhi sought to end discriminatory practices such as the labeling of the members of a certain caste in society as "untouchables."

Gandhi was often imprisoned. He also went on fasts, during which he did not eat for many days, as a form of protest. Gandhi lived, dressed, and ate simply. When religious violence occurred in India, he often visited those places to try to create harmony.

Gandhi was assassinated in 1948, at the age of 78. Yet he still remains one of the most important icons of civil disobedience in history. Because of his work, India became an independent country. He also inspired other people around the world to work for civil rights and freedom.

HUMAN RIGHTS HELPERS

In some countries, civic unrest is extremely dangerous and can lead to imprisonment or death. Citizens in these countries have to rely on outside groups to advocate on their behalf.

The human rights group Amnesty International was formed with a very simple plan: When someone has been unfairly imprisoned for peacefully expressing his or her beliefs, the group will appeal for his or her release. These appeals are usually in the form of letters, which are impartial, nonpartisan, and nonpolitical appeals.

Amnesty International was established in 1961 as a response to the imprisonment of two Portuguese students. It now has more than 3 million supporters in more than 150 countries and territories.

Human Rights Watch is an organization similar to Amnesty International. More than 400 staff members around the world investigate instances of human rights violations and work to change policies that contribute to these violations.

This organization is known for providing accurate, impartial reports about human rights violations around the world. They produce more than 100 reports in 90 different countries, which generate news stories in local and national publications. These stories raise interest and awareness among the people in a position to help victims of abuse and people who may be at risk themselves.

Every year, through Amnesty International's letter-writing campaign, people around the world write hundreds of thousands of letters in support of prisoners who've experienced human rights violations.

In 2011, miners at the Grasberg mine in Papua, Indonesia, went on strike for fair wages. Military troops and police fired shots into the crowd of protesters and killed one person and critically injured another.

Many smaller human rights interest groups have been created in places where human rights are threatened. These are usually where protests or other forms of civic unrest are taking place, such as China, Argentina, and East Timor.

The Advocates for Human Rights is a group dedicated to researching, observing, and changing human rights both in the United States and in foreign countries.

> Their programs have helped women, children, refugees, immigrants, people from ethnic and religious minorities, and other groups of people whose human rights are at risk.

The Advocates for Human Rights raises awareness of human rights situations, works for tolerance, and demands that governments be more accountable for the way they treat their citizens. It has many published resources for use in human rights cases and for monitoring situations. In some ways the Advocates acts as an eye on the state of human rights across the world.

The Advocates for Human Rights does more than teach people about conflict resolution and how to avoid violence. It also monitors global human rights situations and teaches others how to monitor and investigate problems. Encouraging volunteers and training people to work in human rights situations and for reform, it promotes internships around the world in many different types of human rights causes.

WORKERS ACROSS BORDERS

Civic unrest isn't always limited to one country's issues or problems. Sometimes protests and civic action can carry across many national borders, uniting people across the world for a common cause.

The international trade union called IndustriALL is an example of this. IndustriALL was created as a global trade union to represent employees in the mining, energy, and manufacturing trades. It has been especially focused on workers of the Rio Tinto mining company.

Rio Tinto is a global company that operates aluminum, copper, diamond, and iron ore mines all over the world. It has mines in Europe, Africa, Australia, Asia, and North America. Workers claim the company puts profits before people.

> Rio Tinto has a reputation for not treating workers fairly. It has been accused of discriminating against certain workers in terms of wages, expecting workers to work in unsafe conditions, and not operating in a sustainable or environmentally friendly way.

On October 7, 2014, IndustriALL held a Global Day of Action for Rio Tinto employees around the world. From Ulan Bator in Mongolia, it started a worldwide campaign to improve workers' rights.

They held rallies, had meetings where they stopped working for certain parts of the day, and took actions at worksites. These included protesting and putting up signs and banners.

 The People Say

"For far too long, Rio Tinto has systematically put profits before people, sometimes with fatal consequences. Workers are saying enough is enough."

—Kemal Özkan, assistant general secretary of IndustriALL

At the Grasberg copper and gold mine in Indonesia, 38 workers have died in the past two years. IndustriALL took Global Day of Action a step further there and helped workers organize a strike to protest unsafe conditions, such as the tunnel collapse that killed 28 workers.

Workers at the Oyu Tolgoi copper and gold mine in the Gobi Desert of Mongolia also protested unfair dismissals and the fact that Mongolian workers were paid less than workers from other places. Workers accused the company of not following good environmental practices to prevent pollution of land and water, even though it claimed to be environmentally friendly.

The IndustriALL action plan encourages workers to look to each other for support. Their action plans states:

IndustriALL Global Union calls upon all workers and trade unions to unite their forces to build a new movement of global solidarity.

IndustriALL says that its success as a global trade union is partly due to tactics that include building networks and putting pressure on Rio Tinto through the supply chain of other companies that work with it. Using media attention and social networking, as well as careful corporate research are also important.

Perhaps the biggest piece of IndustriALL's success is from workers coming together and creating solidarity no matter what their national borders are or where they live and work. Solidarity is what makes the difference and helps the union achieve goals for the workers.

IndustriALL also has a women's committee that is growing and becoming stronger. They are particularly interested in preventing violence against female workers and achieving maternity protection, so that women who become pregnant don't have to lose their jobs or worry about safety. They also want to train more women to be leaders in the union.

Together with the workers of the Rio Tinto companies, IndustriALL has proved that civic unrest doesn't have to be limited to people in one country or under one government. While many other international human rights causes are supported by people in other countries, IndustriALL actually unites workers who are dealing with the same situations and have a common cause to work together for change.

MALALA WANTS TO GO TO SCHOOL

Children are often victims of human rights violations. Around the world, children are made to work under deplorable, dangerous conditions, because their smaller size makes certain tasks easier to perform. In some regions, children are kept from going to school and getting an education.

Malala Yousafzai didn't think that was right. She lived in Mingora, a town in Swat Valley, in Pakistan's North Western Frontier Province. Her father owned a school and Malala had been encouraged to learn.

When the Taliban took over her village and began to promote the idea that girls shouldn't go to school, Malala did not stay silent. Even though she was only 12 years old, she spoke out.

MALALA YOUSAFZAI

DIARY OF A SCHOOL GIRL

Malala Yousafzai kept a diary about her life as a schoolgirl living in Pakistan, published by BBC Urdu under a pseudonym. The pseudonym was meant to protect Malala from harm, but she still got hurt. You can read excerpts from her diary. How was her life different from the lives of American schoolchildren? Would you have been willing to publish a diary if you were in her situation?

 LESSON

Women represent two-thirds of the 775 million people worldwide who can't read or write. About 55 million girls around the world are unable to go to school.

She kept a diary of her life as a student and it was published by the BBC World Service, a global news organization. In 2009, she wrote:

> *I had a terrible dream yesterday with military helicopters and the Taliban. I have had such dreams since the launch of the military operation in Swat. My mother made me breakfast and I went off to school. I was afraid going to school because the Taliban had issued an edict banning all girls from attending schools. Only 11 students attended the class out of 27. The number decreased because of Taliban's edict.*

Malala kept going to school, even though the military group occupying her village threatened her. This was her form of civic unrest. An act that most children do every day without much thought, Malala chose to do in protest against the Taliban's orders, even when she was afraid.

The Taliban is a radical political group that uses terrorism to control people and to threaten other countries, including the United States. The September 11, 2001, attacks on the World Trade Center in New York City were an act of terrorism carried out by Osama bin Laden's al-Qaeda movement, which the Taliban has been accused of supporting and providing a sanctuary.

Members of this group believe women should not leave their homes without male family members, should not work, and should not go to school. If a woman is found to be wearing fingernail polish, her fingers might be cut off as punishment. If a man refuses to grow a beard, he might be beaten.

The Taliban punishes anyone it feels isn't obeying what it says is Islamic law. However, its members interpret Islam very differently from other people.

Islam is a peaceful religion that states that education is a fundamental necessity for both men and women and that killing is wrong.

The Taliban felt Malala needed to be punished for going to school. In October 2012, Taliban militants shot Malala in the head while she sat on a school bus. She was rushed to England for surgery, which saved her life.

[After a long recuperation, what did Malala want to do? Go back to school.]

She also wanted to make sure that everyone was able to get an education. Since her recovery, Malala has been raising awareness of the importance of education. She was even awarded the Nobel Peace Prize in 2014 for her activism.

The quest for human rights is the most common reason for civic unrest. Around the world, people feel passionate about protecting the basic rights of every person, even when by doing so they put themselves in danger.

KEY QUESTIONS

- **What are some of the reasons people around the world practice civic unrest?**
- **How is civic unrest different in the United States from the rest of the world? How is it the same?**
- **How might the geography of an area affect its human rights policies?**
- **What are some things you can do to help people in other parts of the world?**

At age 17, Malala Yousafzai was the youngest person ever to receive the Nobel Peace Prize for her work as an advocate for girls' education.

THE UMBRELLA REVOLUTION

When British rule of Hong Kong came to an end in 1997, it was decided that for the next 50 years, Hong Kong and China would be considered as one country with two systems of government. But many Hong Kong residents feel that China asserts itself too freely in Hong Kong's elections. In the fall of 2014, tens of thousands of protesters, mostly students, marched in favor of open elections. They used umbrellas to protect themselves from the tear gas released by police, and became known as the Umbrella Movement.

VOCAB LAB

Write down what you think each word means: **human rights, apartheid, treason, corruption, hunger strike, assassinate, advocate, solidarity,** and **conflict resolution.**

Compare your definitions with those of your friends or classmates. Did you all come up with the same meanings? Turn to the text and glossary if you need help.

EQUAL AND LESS EQUAL

A continuing issue in the United States and around the world is the inequality between men and women. Even in the twenty-first century, with all its advancements in women's rights, there are still areas in which the two genders are not treated equally.

- **Identify the different areas where gender inequality is still a problem.** Examples might include politics or salaries in the workplace. Are problems similar in different countries?

- **Research each area and find data concerning the issue.** For example, if you feel that political representation is an important issue, find data about how many women and men hold each type of political office.

- **Create a chart or graph for each area of inequality.** Your chart or graph should be based on the data that you collected.

- **Analyze the data.** Can you say that there is measurable gender inequality in the United States today? If so, where specifically? How about in other countries? Are women and men considered equal and treated equally in South Africa? India? China?

To investigate more, research gender inequality in the early twentieth century, before suffrage, and again later in the twentieth century, such as in the 1960s and 1970s. What trends can you find? How does this data compare to today's data? Are there areas in which women have gained or lost equality?

JOINING IN AND LENDING YOUR VOICE

When people work together, they have a greater chance of changing the world. You can do this right in your own community.

- **Research a nonprofit group that shows a great deal of civic involvement.** The group might be a branch of a national organization or something more specific to your area.

- **Review its mission and the issues it helps with.** Do you agree with it? Is this important to you? What kind of activities does the group offer?

- **Find out if this nonprofit has opportunities for students to become involved.** If the group does not usually include student participation, create a plan or proposal to encourage student involvement and present it to the group. If the group already has opportunities for students, create a presentation for your class about the group and encourage them to participate. Include the group's mission, what they do, and how students can help.

To investigate more, think about a nonprofit you would like to create. What problem do you see that your nonprofit could work to solve? Use your talents, such as drawing, painting, telling stories, or writing poetry or songs, and create something to express your feelings about that problem. You can design a poster calling attention to an issue, write a song that someone might sing during a protest, or draft a letter protesting injustice. Your goal is to draw attention to an issue in a way that people will notice and remember.

RAISE YOUR VOICES AND YOUR HANDS...

YOUR TURN

No matter what the cause, the techniques of civil disobedience can be very effective. Now it's your turn to give it a try.

- **Identify a cause that's very important to you, your family, your school, or your community.** It should be one that can only be changed through some level of government. It might be something local such as a proposed use for a new community building in your hometown. Or it could be part of a larger issue such as requiring recycling and composting throughout your state. Choosing a local cause is the best way to get started and get results.

- **Organize a rally or march about your cause.** What would you like people to know? What specific actions are you asking your government to take? Choose a time and place for your rally or march, then advertise it using posters, fliers, newspapers, and social media.

- **Make sure you follow the rules.** You may need a permit from your town or city or permission from your school to hold a rally or gathering.

- **Make sure that your communication is clear and easy to read.** What is the rally for? When and where will it take place? Why is it important for people to attend? Are you asking people to sign a petition or asking them to vote a certain way in an upcoming election? What are the positive and negative outcomes if this change is or isn't made?

- **Don't forget to clean up after the rally.** You want everyone remembering your cause, not the mess you left. Take pictures and post them after the rally is over to further support your cause.

> To investigate more, follow up on media coverage of your issue. Did the community vote on it? Did it pass and create the change you were seeking or was it defeated? What might have helped the issue succeed or fail? What would you do differently next time?

WHICH PROTEST WORKS BEST?

By now you know that there are many different ways of protesting, from small, peaceful rallies to huge demonstrations. But what works best?

- Within a group, list as many different kinds of protest activities as you can. Sort them by type: violent, nonviolent, illegal, legal, small scale, large scale, et cetera.

- With all of these types of protest in mind, discuss the role of protest in a democracy. What does it accomplish? Is it necessary? Could it be replaced with something else?

- Now discuss which types of protest are acceptable in a democracy. Should they always be peaceful? Is violence ever acceptable? Does one form of protest work better than another? Why? Is there any form of protest that should never take place in a democracy?

- Can you determine from your research which forms of protest in a democracy are most effective? Which are the most damaging?

> To investigate more, research protests in the news today. How do these specific examples from current events illustrate your points? Can you find events in history to support your ideas?

IN THE NEWS

In 2014, there were many protests in Ukraine over the government the country should have. People spoke out against corruption and questioned whether part of Ukraine would become part of Russia.

* **Using news reports and social media, research the events in Ukraine.** What are the different types of protests that were used in Ukraine from late 2013 through 2014?

* **For each protest, collect media images and quotes about that particular incident.** Use them to create a collage that shows the course of the protest movements in Ukraine.

* **Now analyze your images.** What is being conveyed through these images or words, particularly to other parts of the world? Is one particular side of the issue (pro-democracy Ukrainians, pro-Russia supporters, pro-Ukraine government) being conveyed more than others? What conclusions can you draw about the effects of media images and social media on the way the world views incidents of civil unrest?

To investigate more, choose a cause to research. It can be one from history, such as women's suffrage, the Civil Rights movement, or apartheid. You can also choose a current issue that you feel strongly about. Is there a story of injustice or of a human rights violation that is in the news right now? Collect media images and quotes, then create a collage that expresses how you feel about the issue.

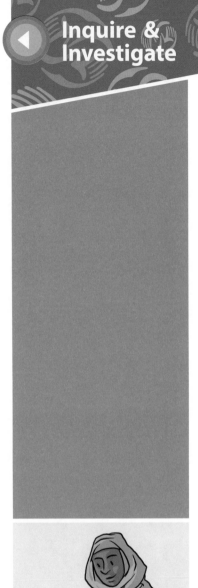

Chapter 6 ▶
Technology and Democracy

What role does technology play in a democracy?

Technology can help both established and emerging democracies by allowing better communication.

Not that long ago, civic unrest and protest movements relied on word of mouth and traditional media sources such as newspapers and television to spread their messages. If the protest was small and localized, it might not get much attention. Its goals might not be achieved.

All that has changed, however, because of the Internet and the rise of social media. Now it is easy to post updates and images about protest movements on social media sites such as Facebook and Twitter, and to create new websites that highlight those movements. Information posted on the World Wide Web is instantly accessible anywhere people have Internet access or cell phone service. People can respond, repost, and share the information immediately. Local protests can quickly become national and even global events.

But there's more to the effects of technology on democracy than just spreading the news about protests and other events. Technology is changing the democratic process itself.

POWER TO THE (ORDINARY) PEOPLE

Many political experts feel that the Internet has made it even easier for ordinary people to influence and change the political process. Both the process of electing people to government offices and the ways government actually works are now different. People can become active in politics through digital avenues such as political blogs, social networking sites, online media versions of newspapers and magazines, instant news coverage, and video sharing.

> Because of the Internet, anyone can make his or her political views known and provide support for a candidate, all without having to leave home.

Technology also makes it easier to run political campaigns. Candidates are able to raise money more efficiently. Lesser-known campaigns can gain support now that many voters get their news and information online as well. Word of mouth travels at the speed of bytes when people show their support on their personal social media sites or on a candidate's or organization's web pages.

And as we've seen, the Internet makes it easier for people in a democracy to protest and share those viewpoints with others. On the Internet, anyone can create groups and foster change in government policies and organizations. Civic unrest is more effective because of the Internet's ability to reach a wide audience instantly.

Civic LESSON

Eighty-five percent of adult Americans now use the Internet, but Internet use is lower with older Americans. Only about half of those older than 65 use the Internet.

During protests in Egypt in 2011, tweets from citizens about political change increased from about 2,300 a day to 230,000 a day.

People who have easy access to computers and the Internet have an advantage over those who don't when it comes to participation in government.

However, there are people who feel that technology may actually endanger democracy. Twitter, texting, and comments on other forms of social media are instantaneous, but real world public issues can't be fully represented by quick video sound bites or within Twitter's 140 characters. The voters may only get brief slogans rather than thoughtful comments about a candidate's position.

Critics also worry that candidates can be elected because they and their staff are good at creating these quick sound bites. Will voters judge them by their online presence rather than their experience and knowledge? How might this affect the future?

Another concern is that information travels so quickly that people in government may not have enough time to reflect on a decision or a quote before it is shared all over the world. Citizens might have shorter attention spans because of the speed of the Internet, where issues quickly become trends and then fade away.

> The other negative part of technology in the democratic process is that access to that technology is unevenly distributed. Not everyone has the same access to computers and the Internet.

According to the U.S. census of 2012, between 20 and 25 percent of U.S. households were still without access to the Internet. Studies have shown that most of the people without Internet access in their homes make less than $30,000 a year and are older than 65 years. People in those households have to rely on traditional methods of getting information about their government, such as print publications. Or they have to travel somewhere, such as their local libraries, to access the information on a computer.

> Lack of Internet access makes it harder to participate in social media threads about protest and political group activities.

Some people might be unfairly excluded from participating as much as other groups. As the ability to be online plays a bigger and bigger role in accessing information and supporting candidates and special interest groups, it might create a shift in who is protesting and who is not.

WHAT HAPPENED IN FERGUSON?

Social media sites such as Facebook, Twitter, Instagram, and Snapchat have affected the way people receive news about events of civic unrest. This was the case in Ferguson, Missouri, a suburb of St. Louis, when an unarmed African American teenager named Michael Brown was shot and killed by a white police officer. Later, a grand jury came to the conclusion that the police officer was not to be indicted.

Both the actual event and the grand jury's decision sparked protests in the Ferguson area and in other cities. How? Through social media. Instead of waiting for traditional news sources to report on the events, people read posts and tweets about on-the-ground experiences and watched shared videos of events unfolding on the streets of Ferguson.

FIRST AMENDMENT RIGHTS

On August 15, 2014, President Barack Obama issued a statement that said: "There is never an excuse for violence against police, or for those who would use this tragedy as a cover for vandalism or looting. There's also no excuse for police to use excessive force against peaceful protests, or to throw protesters in jail for lawfully exercising their First Amendment rights. And here, in the United States of America, police should not be bullying or arresting journalists who are just trying to do their jobs and report to the American people on what they see on the ground."

PS

Many people were spurred to take part in the protests by traveling to Missouri or joining with like-minded people in their own cities. Los Angeles, New York City, and Atlanta all experienced forms of civic unrest in reaction to what happened in Ferguson, Missouri.

The methods of social media can spill over into face-to-face communication. One popular Twitter hashtag to arise is #blacklivesmatter. This hashtag began popping up after the white man who had killed another young black man, Trayvon Martin, was acquitted in Florida.

Twitter users can search for tweets with that hashtag to find information about racial issues, events, and support. This slogan has even made its way beyond social media sites. In Boston, Massachusetts, prisoners displayed signs with this saying in the windows of the South Bay Detention Center during the Ferguson protests.

[**Is social media a good thing or a bad thing for civic unrest?**]

Information is a key component in affecting social change. But not everyone has the general population's best interest in mind. Some people have used protests as opportunities for looting and causing damage.

Social media lets people organize immediately after an event to make the biggest impact, but this might mean that protesters don't have all the information they need to make informed decisions. Information that travels at the speed of bytes isn't always correct.

The protests and riots in Ferguson were both peaceful and violent. But they shared the idea that citizens of a democracy have the right to protest when they feel they are being treated unfairly. The Ferguson events drew people from all over the country who wanted to add their voices to the force of civic unrest.

SECURITY VERSUS TRANSPARENCY

In 2013, a former Central Intelligence Agency and National Security Agency employee named Edward Snowden released thousands of classified government documents to the media. He used a site called WikiLeaks, which is a nonprofit media organization started in 2007 by Julian Assange, an Australian publisher and journalist. Snowdon was charged with stealing government property and espionage, and is currently living in Russia under political asylum.

The purpose of WikiLeaks is to bring important news and information to the public. People are encouraged to leak information to WikiLeaks through a tip box on their website that is anonymous. WikiLeaks then publishes the leaked material alongside mainstream news stories about the same subject matter to show the real truth behind the news that people usually read.

[The people who operate WikiLeaks feel they are performing a vital service. What do you think?]

WIKILEAKS PROCLAMATION

"Publishing improves transparency, and this transparency creates a better society for all people. Better scrutiny leads to reduced corruption and stronger democracies in all society's institutions, including government, corporations and other organizations. A healthy, vibrant and inquisitive journalistic media plays a vital role in achieving these goals. We are part of that media."

—WikiLeaks website

Snowden's leak of classified documents has been called the biggest leak of government materials in U.S. history. Some people have called him a hero and a patriot, while others view him as a traitor or a dissident. Many people applaud him as a whistleblower who has brought attention to issues such as government surveillance and secrecy.

Snowden has raised an important question: What is the proper balance between national security and information privacy?

PREDICTING THE FUTURE

When is it a good thing to release information that might lead to a change in government, and when does it threaten the security of the country? The U.S. Department of Defense has launched several research studies to examine the dynamics of civic unrest.

It wants to know when and why civic unrest becomes potentially dangerous. The world may face more moments of protest as water shortages, climate change, and other issues become more serious.

> World governments want to be prepared for larger episodes of civic unrest while looking into the conditions, characteristics, and consequences of political protests.

Researchers have discovered that they might be able to predict civic unrest using computers. They entered data from news articles between 1979 and 2011, both positive and negative, and identified patterns that led to periods of unrest. The computer program not only looked at the tone of the news articles, but how that tone changed through time.

Eventually, this computer program may be able to predict episodes of unrest before they happen, based on what it sees in the news from around the world. How could this kind of program help governments serve their citizens? Could this information be used against a country's citizens?

COMMUNICATION

Technology also has an effect on how a democratic government communicates with its people. In most cases, technology has made it easier for people to get information about their government. If you want to be educated about various processes, governing groups, and laws, as well as perform some of the tasks that are part of living in a democracy, technology can help you.

To find out who your congressperson is, you can locate the answer with just a few clicks on a government website. If you want to get a passport to travel or find out if there are any travel advisories for places where your government might need to protect you, it's as easy as finding the right government website.

Technology makes the government more efficient when it comes to providing instant news and information to citizens in times of conflict or emergency.

Technology can smooth the way for processes that are important to a successful democracy, making it possible for the positive effects of citizen involvement and government transparency to be available right away.

The People Say

"Our evidence suggests that social media carried a cascade of messages about freedom and democracy across North Africa and the Middle East, and helped raise expectations for the success of political uprising. People who shared interest in democracy built extensive social networks and organized political action. Social media became a critical part of the toolkit for greater freedom."

—Philip Howard, associate professor in communication at the University of Washington

The government can quickly and easily post any kind of information for its citizens, from alerts and warnings to basic information and historical documents from American history. It's equally easy for citizens to contact their government representatives using email.

In places where democracy is new and governments are trying to create a stable and strong democratic government, technology can be vital. First, the Internet can be used by activists and reformers to help get a country to the point of democracy, and help it form a successful government. It gives the people a voice and a power that they may never have had before. Technology may also help the new government be open and transparent—it can post its policies and rules online, where they can be accessed immediately.

In both established and new democracies, technology improves communication and efficiency. It also strengthens democratic processes, such as voting and communicating with political leaders. It can improve the quality of news and information, since it can come quickly and directly from the government, instead of finding its way to the people through news media and other means that might distort or change the message.

TECHNOLOGY AND CITIZEN ADVOCATES

Technology has influenced how citizen advocates play their roles in a democracy. A citizen advocate is someone who represents a group of other citizens and their interests to the government or other decision-making group. Lobbyists, who talk to politicians about specific issues, are citizen advocates. They are usually actively working for a change in policy or position in the government.

Citizen advocates' roles have changed because of technology. Now, an organization working for a specific change of policy can use volunteers and technology to contact government officials on the organization's behalf, transmitting messages that the organization provides to them. This is called voter advocacy.

> Democracy and technology can work together to create stronger and more open relationships between the people and their government.

Whether used within a democracy that's old and established or new and emerging, technology gives the average person the ability to communicate, become educated, and lend his or her voice to that government more effectively than ever before. What about civic unrest, and the rights of people to make their voices heard and create change where change is needed? Technology is another piece of the process that every democracy provides its citizens just by virtue of what it is: a government by the people and for the people.

KEY QUESTIONS

- **How is technology used by activists during times of civic unrest? How is it used by governments?**

- **Is social media a good thing or a bad thing for society? Does it help or hurt the relationships between citizens and institutions such as the police or government?**

GRASSROOTS AND GRASSTOPS

When it comes to getting citizens to participate in their government, there are two terms that public affairs experts use. *Grassroots* refers to getting average Americans to communicate with their elected officials. *Grasstops* refers to motivating more influential Americans, such as local elected officials and business leaders, to contact politicians.

Civic LESSON

It is estimated that in 2012, industries and special interest groups spent $6.7 billion on lobbyists who worked in Washington, DC, to influence Congressional members. These trained advocates, who can personalize their communication according to the person they're talking to, can also use technological tools to be more effective.

WHO'S TWEET IS BETTER?

Using Twitter has become an acceptable, if not required, form of communication, even for the president of the United States.

VOCAB LAB

Write down what you think each word means: **media, social media, slogans, anonymous, transparency, dissident, whistleblower, espionage, political asylum,** and **citizen advocates.**

Compare your definitions with those of your friends or classmates. Did you all come up with the same meanings? Turn to the text and glossary if you need help.

- **Find the Twitter feed for the president of the United States.** What kinds of things does the president tweet about? Does he have a lot of followers? Do you think he has as many followers as a rock star? Is this kind of communication a good thing or a bad thing in terms of quality? Why or why not?

- **Find Twitter feeds for another government leader—the head of state for another country would be a great one to find.** How do they differ from the president's tweets? How are they similar? Do you think they make that leader seem more accessible?

- **Think about the influence of Twitter feeds and other social media outlets.** What does this say about the ability of the average American to influence his or her fellow citizens with opinions and viewpoints? What are the positive and negative aspects of this?

To investigate more, write your own messages using only 140 characters about an issue you have a passion for. You can do this on paper or in a word document instead of signing up for Twitter. How is this different from writing a whole paragraph? Can you express yourself more or less easily?

TWEETS REPLIES PHOTOS

COMPOSE NEW TWEET ✕

WHOOPS, GOT A LITTLE TOO EXCITED IN THAT LAST TWEET. THAT 140-CHARACTER LIMIT IS A HARSH MISTRESS, HUH?

ADD PHOTO   37 TWEET

HEY, IT'S ME @HEYITSME
OKAY, FIRST POST (OR SHOULD I SAY TWEET?). MY FRIENDS KEEP BOTHERING ME TO SIGN UP SO IF YOU GUYS ARE READING THIS, YOU WIN! I'M REALLY EXC

WHERE IS YOUR NEWS COMING FROM?

Different news media report the news in different ways. Your understanding about events can be altered according to where you're getting your news.

- **Choose a current event that has taken place within the past six months to a year.** Find a selection of reports about that event from a variety of sources, including traditional newspapers and magazines, online sources, social media, and blogs. Compare the various reports, and note how long after the event they were published or posted.

- **Compare the ways traditional news outlets and online outlets covered this event.** Which seemed to reach the public more quickly? Was one more thoughtful than the other? More vivid? Which seemed to be more accurate about the event? Did one have more personal opinion and less objectivity?

Research an election in American history where the media actually predicted an incorrect outcome, or made a premature prediction. To start, look at the 1948 election between Thomas Dewey and Harry S. Truman, or the 2000 election between George W. Bush and Al Gore. How do you think this affected the public's feelings about the event, or about voting?

FINDING INFORMATION . . . EASILY

Using the tools of technology, finding important information from your government should be quick and easy. Try this scavenger hunt!

- **Divide into several teams.** Each team needs to have its own computer.

- **Find each of the following items of information.** Use only U.S. government sites ending in .gov.

  1. A recent travel advisory for somewhere else in the world

  2. Five key facts about hurricane preparedness

  3. Who your congressional representative is and how to contact him or her

  4. How to apply for a U.S. passport

  5. Who is eligible to vote in the United States and how to register to vote in your area

- **Once you have found this information, have a teacher or librarian verify that it is correct.** The first group to finish the list AND have the correct answers is the winner!

To investigate more, search websites that aren't owned by the government. Do you find any incorrect or misleading information? What sort of websites offer poor quality information? What should you think about when considering sources for research?

abuse of power: using power to hurt other people.

activist: a person who fights for something he or she believes in.

advocate: a person who publicly supports a particular cause or policy.

agenda: a list of things to be done.

amendment: a change or addition to a motion, bill, or constitution.

American Civil Liberties Union: a nonprofit organization that works to ensure the civil rights of all U.S. citizens.

American Revolution: the 1775 to 1783 war during which the 13 American colonies fought England for independence.

anarchist: a person who does not believe that government and laws are necessary, and wants to abolish them.

anecdote: a short story about a real person or event.

annex: to take possession or control of something.

apartheid: a policy of segregation and discrimination based on race.

aristocrat: someone who belongs to the upper levels of society.

assassinate: to kill a leader.

asylum: protection granted by a country or government to refugees from another country.

authoritarian: favoring complete obedience to authority instead of individual freedoms.

ballot: a piece of paper on which people write their votes.

BCE: put after a date, BCE stands for Before Common Era and counts years down to zero. CE stands for Common Era and counts years up from zero. This book was published in 2015 CE.

bill: a draft of a proposed law that is presented to a legislature for discussion.

bill of rights: a document that spells out some of the rights that belong to the citizens of a country.

Boston Tea Party: the December 16, 1773, act of protest against the Tea Act. A group of colonists disguised themselves as Native Americans, boarded British ships, and dumped British tea into Boston Harbor.

boycott: to refuse to buy, use, or participate in something as a way to protest.

campaign: a connected series of activities designed to bring about a result, such as electing a person to public office or selling a product to a large number of people.

candidate: a person who runs for an office in the government.

case: a dispute between opposing parties that is resolved by a court or other legal process.

catalyst: an event or person who causes a change.

censor: when the government blocks citizens from seeing certain information.

checks and balances: a system of three branches of government in which no one branch becomes too powerful. Each branch can be restrained by the other two.

child labor: putting children to work in industry or business and depriving them of an education.

citizen: a person who legally belongs to a country and has the rights and protection of that country.

citizen advocate: a person who actively works toward a policy change.

civic: relating to duty and responsibility to community.

civic engagement: actively participating to make a difference in one's community and country.

civic unrest: demonstrations organized to disrupt the usual flow of business to bring awareness to specific causes. Also call civil unrest.

civil disobedience: refusing to obey certain laws or pay taxes as a peaceful form of political protest.

civil rights: the rights that every person should have regardless of his or her gender, race, or religion.

civilian: a person who is not in the military.

GLOSSARY

civilization: a community of people that is advanced in art, science, and government.

classified: officially secret.

collective: done by people acting as a group.

collective bargaining: negotiations between an employer and a labor union, usually on wages and working conditions.

colonist: a settler living in a new land.

colony: a country or area that is under the part or full political control of another country.

communism: an economy in which the government owns everything used in the production and distribution of goods.

communist: someone who follows the beliefs of communism, which is a system of government based on the holding of all property in common.

compromise: an agreement reached by two sides working together.

conflict: a period of disagreement that sometimes includes violence.

conflict resolution: peacefully resolving a disagreement by making sure each side has at least some of its needs met.

conformity: behavior that is similar to the behavior of most of the people in a group.

Congress: a group of people who represent the states and make laws for the country.

consensus: a general agreement.

consent: permission or approval for something to happen.

consequence: the result of an event or condition.

conservative: a person who dislikes change and holds to traditional values and attitudes, especially in politics.

constituent: a person who lives and votes in an area.

constitution: the written system of beliefs and laws by which a country, state, or organization is governed.

constitutional monarchy: a form of government in which a king or queen acts as head of state but is legally guided by a written or unwritten constitution and an elected body of politicians.

consumerism: a willingness to spend money on goods and services.

controversy: an argument that involves many people who strongly disagree.

corporate: relating to a large company.

correlation: a connection or relationship between two or more things.

corrupt: the dishonest or illegal behavior of people in power.

counterprotester: a protester who stands against other protesters.

counterrevolutionary: acting or speaking out against a revolution.

court: a place where trials and other legal cases happen, usually presided over by a judge.

critically: involving careful examination and judgment.

declaration of independence: an announcement to the world that a new country has formed. The U.S. Declaration of Independence was written in 1776 to explain why America was separating itself from Britain and becoming its own country.

defendant: a person accused of a crime.

defender: a person who defends someone or something.

delegate: a person authorized to represent others, especially at a conference or political assembly.

democracy: a system of government where the people choose who will represent and govern them.

Democrat: a member of the Democratic Party, which typically believes in a broader reach of government.

democratic: supporting democracy and its principles of freedom.

demonstrate: to publicly display dissatisfaction.

destabilize: to cause unrest or keep something such as a government from operating in the normal way.

dictator: a ruler with total control over a country, particularly one who has gotten that power through force.

dictatorship: a government by a dictator with absolute rule over the people.

discriminate: to unfairly treat a person or group differently from others, usually because of their race, gender, or age.

disempower: to make a person or group less powerful or confident.

disorder: a state of confusion and disruption.

disruption: a major disturbance that interrupts the usual order of things.

dissent: to disagree with a widely held opinion.

dissident: a person who disagrees with a widely held opinion.

dynamics: the pattern of activity in an event.

economic: having to do with the resources and wealth of a country.

editorial: a newspaper article that gives an opinion.

election: a vote where citizens choose a leader.

election fraud: illegal interference with the process of an election.

elector: a person who has the right to vote in an election.

electoral college: a group of electors chosen by people in each state to formally vote for the president and vice president.

eligible: able to be chosen for something.

enforce: to carry out a law.

environmentalist: a person who works to protect the natural world from pollution and other threats.

equal rights: the idea that all people have the same rights and freedoms.

equality: the quality of being equal.

espionage: using spies to obtain information about foreign countries.

ethnic: sharing customs, languages, and beliefs.

ethnic group: people with common ancestors sharing customs, languages, and beliefs.

European Union: a political and economic union of 28 members, mostly in Europe.

execute: to carry out the death sentence of a person found guilty of a crime.

executive: the person or branch of government responsible for putting policies or laws into effect.

eyewitness: a person who sees an act or event and can give a firsthand account of it.

faction: a small, organized group within a larger group, party, government, or organization.

fair trade: trade in which fair prices are paid to producers in developing countries.

famine: a period of great hunger and lack of food for a large population.

federal republic: a form of government made up of a group of states, governed by a constitution.

figurehead: a leader without real power.

First Continental Congress: a group of delegates from the American colonies who met in 1774 to discuss what to do about England.

force: to make someone do something.

foreigner: a person from another country.

Founding Fathers: members of the Constitutional Convention.

framework: a basic plan, form, or outline that supports something else.

fraud: the crime of using dishonest methods to take something valuable away from someone else.

free trade: unrestricted trade between countries.

freedom: the ability to choose and act without constraints.

freedoms: specific actions people are able to choose, such as speech and religion.

French Revolution: a period of violent change in France between 1789 and 1799.

GLOSSARY

garment trade: factories and stores that make and sell cloth goods, such as clothes.

gender: male or female.

general election: a regular election for state or national offices.

globalization: the tendency of businesses, technologies, or philosophies to spread throughout the world.

government: an organization or system that controls a city, state, or country.

grievance: a real or imagined wrong that is a cause for complaint or protest, especially when it has to do with being treated unfairly.

guillotine: a device that uses a heavy blade to cut off a person's head.

harmony: peace and agreement.

heredity: the process of passing something from parents to children.

hierarchy: a system of people or things that are ranked or divided according to levels.

human rights: the rights that belong to all people, such as freedom from torture, the right to live, and freedom from slavery.

humane: with compassion.

humanitarian: having to do with helping the welfare or happiness of people.

hunger strike: a form of protest in which protesters refuse to eat until their demands have been met.

icon: a widely recognized symbol of a certain time, or a person or thing that grows to represent a larger idea.

ideology: a set of opinions or beliefs.

immigrant: a person who leaves his or her own country to live in another country.

impartial: fair, without bias or prejudice.

impeach: to formally charge a public official with a crime or misconduct.

incite: to stir up, encourage, or urge on.

independent: free from outside control.

inequality: differences in opportunity and treatment based on social, ethnic, racial, or economic qualities.

inferior: lower in rank or status.

injustice: unfair action or treatment.

insane asylum: an institution for people with mental illness.

instantaneous: occurring, done, or completed in an instant.

interpret: to determine the meaning of something.

intimidation: the act of making another person fearful with threats or other shows of power.

issue: a subject of concern.

judicial: having to do with the branch of government that interprets laws and administers justice.

juror: someone who is part of a jury.

justice: fair action or treatment based on the law.

labor union: a group of workers that bargains with the people they work for. Also called a trade union.

law: a formal system of rules to govern behavior.

lawlessness: not regulated or controlled by law.

legislation: new laws.

legislative: having to do with the branch of government that makes or changes laws.

legitimacy: meeting the requirements of the law.

liberal: a person who is open to change and new ideas and believes that government should actively support social and political change.

libertarian: a person who believes that people should be allowed to do and say what they want without any interference from the government or authorities.

lobby: to try to influence legislators on an issue.

lobbyist: a person who tries to influence legislators on behalf of a special interest, business, or cause.

lottery: a random selection.

majority: more than half of the people or voters.

martyr: a person who commits suicide for his or her religious beliefs.

mass opinion: the collective opinion of many people on one issue.

means of production: the physical tools used in production, such as machinery, factories, ships, and raw materials.

media: the industry in the business of presenting news to the public by methods including radio, television, Internet, and newspapers.

militia: a group of citizens who are trained to fight but who only serve in time of emergency.

minority: a group of people, such as African Americans, that is smaller than or different from the larger group. Also less than half of the people or voters.

monarch: a hereditary leader, such as a king, queen, or emperor, who rules a country.

monarchy: a government ruled by a monarch.

movement: a group of people working together to advance their shared political ideas.

negotiate: to reach an agreement, compromise, or treaty through bargaining and discussing.

nobility: in the past, the people considered to be the most important in a society.

nonpartisan: free from any connection to political parties.

nonprofit: an organization supported by donations whose main mission is to help people, animals, the environment, or other causes.

nonviolent: characterized by not using physical force or power.

occupation: the seizure and control of an area.

official: a person who holds public office and has official duties.

oppression: an unjust or cruel exercise of authority and power.

parliament: in some governments, the group of people responsible for making laws.

participate: to take part in.

patriot: a person who is passionate about supporting his or her country.

peace march: a protest march against war and in favor of peace.

peasant: a farmer in feudal society who lived on and farmed land owned by his lord.

pending: awaiting a decision or settlement.

persecute: to treat someone cruelly or unfairly, especially because of religion, race, or political beliefs.

persecution: harm or suffering inflicted on someone because they are different.

petition: to make a formal request to an authority when it relates to a particular cause.

philosopher: someone who thinks about and questions the way things are in the world.

picket: to stand or march near a certain place to protest or persuade others not to enter.

policy: an action or rule adopted by a country.

political: relating to running a government and holding onto power.

political convention: a meeting of a political party to select candidates.

political party: a group that holds particular ideas about how to run the government.

poll: a collection of opinions on a particular subject for the purpose of analysis. Also the place where people vote.

popular vote: the vote for a candidate made by qualified voters, as opposed to the vote made by the elected representatives.

power: the ability to direct the behavior of other people or events.

preamble: an introduction to a document that states the reasons for creating it.

prejudice: an unfair feeling of dislike for a person or group, usually based on gender, race, or religion.

press: the news media.

primary election: an election that narrows the field of candidates before an election for office.

GLOSSARY

primary source: an original document or physical object created during the event or time period being studied.

prime minister: the head of government in a parliamentary system.

privilege: a right or benefit that is given to some people but not to others.

procedure: a series of actions performed in a specific order.

propaganda: ideas or statements that are sometimes exaggerated or even false. They are spread to help a cause, political leader, or government.

prosecutor: a lawyer who represents the state or the people in a criminal trial.

protest: to object to something, often in public.

protest march: an expression of opposition through marching.

pseudonym: a false name adopted by someone to conceal his or her identity.

public assembly: a group of people gathered for a specific purpose.

publicity: the process of gaining public attention.

punishment: a penalty imposed for a real or imagined offense.

race: a group of people that shares distinct physical qualities, such as skin color.

racist: hatred of people of a different race.

radical: a person with extreme political or social views.

rally: to call together for a common goal.

ratify: to give official approval of something, such as a constitutional amendment.

rebel: to fight against authority. Also a person fighting against authority.

rebellion: an act of open or violent resistance.

reelection: to be chosen again by means of voting.

reform: the improvement of wrong or bad conditions.

refugee: a person forced to leave his or her native land to seek safety, usually as a result of war or persecution.

regulate: to control by rules or laws.

renounce: to give up.

representation: a person or group that speaks or acts for or in support of another person or group.

representative: a single person who speaks for the wishes of a group.

republic: a kind of government with elected officials.

Republican: a member of the Republican Party, which typically believes in less government and stronger states rights.

resources: something a country has that supports its wealth, such as oil, water, food, money, and land.

revolt: to fight against a government or person of authority.

revolution: when the people overthrow the government.

rights: that which is due to a person naturally or legally.

riot: a gathering of people protesting something, which gets out of control and violent.

sanctions: threatened penalties for disobeying a law or rule, usually imposed on a country by another country.

Second Continental Congress: delegates from the American colonies who met beginning in 1775 to discuss whether or not America should declare its independence.

secondary source: a document or recording that offers or discusses information originally found elsewhere.

segregation: the practice of keeping people of different races, genders, or religions separate from each other.

sentiment: a view, attitude, feeling, or emotion toward a situation or event.

short-term: occurring over a short period of time.

sit-in: a form of protest in which people occupy a space and refuse to move.

slave: a person owned by another person and forced to work without pay.

slogan: a phrase used by a business or other group to get attention.

sniper: a skilled shooter who shoots at other people from a concealed place.

social: living in groups.

social media: online communities where people share information, ideas, and opinions, often in real time, such as Facebook, Twitter, and Instagram.

society: an organized community of people.

solidarity: a feeling of unity between people who have the same interests and goals.

special interest group: a group of people that strongly supports a particular cause.

status: the position of someone in a group.

strike: when everyone walks off the job to protest working conditions or pay.

suffrage: the right to vote, especially in a political election.

surveillance: observing an enemy.

sustainable: something that can be maintained at a certain level or rate.

sweatshop: a factory or workshop where people work long hours in poor conditions and for low pay.

symbol: something that is important because of what it stands for or represents.

system of government: the way a government is structured.

tactics: a carefully planned action or strategy to achieve something.

tax: money charged by a government.

technology: tools, methods, and systems used to solve a problem or do work.

tolerance: the willingness to accept behavior and beliefs that are different from your own.

totalitarian: a system of government that has absolute control over its people and requires them to be completely obedient.

trade: the buying, selling, or exchange of goods and services between countries.

trade agreement: when two or more nations agree on the terms of trade between them.

trade union: a group of workers that bargains with the people they work for. Also called a labor union.

transparent: being open and honest, not having secrets.

treason: actions that go against one's own country.

treaty: an agreement between two or more countries.

troops: soldiers.

Twitter: an online service that allows users to send and read messages called tweets.

tyrannical: exercising power in a cruel, harsh, or oppressive way.

universal: used or understood by everyone.

unjust: not fair.

unwieldy: difficult to handle, control, or deal with because of being large, heavy, or complex.

violence: physical force intended to hurt, damage, or kill someone or something.

vote: an expression of choice in an election or poll.

voter registration: the requirement of voters to sign up with an official registry in order to vote.

whistleblower: a person who informs on an individual or company that is breaking the law.

RESOURCES

◉ BOOKS

Bright-Moore, Susan. *What Is a Democracy?*
St. Catharine's, Ontario: Crabtree Publishing, 2013.

Friedman, Lauri S. *Democracy.*
Farmington Hills, MI: Greenhaven Press, 2008.

Friedman, Mark. *The Democratic Process.*
New York, NY: Scholastic, 2012.

Gelletly, Leeanne et al. *Major Forms of World Government: Democracy, Communism, Dictatorship, Fascism, Milestones, Monarchy, Oligarchy, Theocracy.*
Broomall, PA: Mason Crest, 2013.

Gutman, Dan. *Election! A Kid's Guide to Picking Our President.*
New York, NY: Open Road Media, 2012.

Hardyman, Robyn. *Understanding Political Systems: What Is a Democracy?*
New York, NY: Gareth Stevens Publishing, 2014.

Hort, Lenny. *DK Biography: Nelson Mandela.*
New York, NY: DK Publishing, 2006.

Hunter, Nick. *Understanding Political Systems: What is a Dictatorship?*
New York, NY: Gareth Stevens Publishing, 2014.

Hynes, Patricia. *Citizens and Their Governments: Rights and Values.*
North Mankato, MN: Cherry Lake Publishing, 2007.

Jackson, Carolyn. *The Election Book: The People Pick a President.*
New York, NY: Scholastic, 2012.

Judson, Karen. *The United States Constitution: Its History, Bill of Rights, and Amendments.*
Berkeley Heights, NJ: Enslow Publishers, 2012.

Kenney, Karen Latchana. *Understanding Political Systems: What is a Parliamentary Government?*
New York, NY: Gareth Stevens Publishing, 2014.

Kenney, Karen Latchana. *Understanding Political Systems: What is Communism?*
New York, NY: Gareth Stevens Publishing, 2014.

Kirk, Andrew. *Understanding Thoreau's "Civil Disobedience."*
New York, NY: Rosen Publishing, 2010.

Koosmann, Melissa. *The Fall of Apartheid in South Africa.*
Hockessin, DE: Mitchell Lane Publishing, 2009.

Kowalski, Kathiann M. *Checks and Balances: A Look at the Powers of Government.*
Minneapolis, MN: Lerner Publishing Group, 2012.

Leavitt, Amie Jane. *Who Really Created Democracy?*
Mankato, MN: Fact Finders, 2011.

Liljeblad, Fredrik. *Citizens and Their Governments: Democracy at Work.*
North Mankato, MN: Cherry Lake Publishing, 2013.

Lusted, Marcia Amidon. *Essential Events: Tiananmen Square Protests.*
Minneapolis, MN: Abdo Publishing, 2010.

Mara, Wil. *Civil Unrest in the 1960s: Riots and Their Aftermath.*
New York, NY: Cavendish Square Publishing, 2009.

Rees, Peter. *Liberty: Blessing or Burden?*
Danbury, CT: Children's Press, 2007.

Steele, Philip. *Vote.*
New York, NY: DK Publishing, 2008.

Swain, Gwenyth. *Documents of Freedom: A Look at the Declaration of Independence, the Bill of Rights, and the U.S. Constitution.*
Minneapolis, MN: Lerner Publishing Group, 2012.

Thomas, William David. *What is a Constitution?*
New York, NY: Gareth Stevens Publishing, 2008.

Wilkinson, Philip. *World History Biographies: Gandhi: The Young Protester Who Founded a Nation.*
Washington, DC: National Geographic Children's Publishing, 2007.

▶ WEBSITES

PBS Kids Democracy Project
pbskids.org/democracy
Information, games, and activities about democracy and government in the United States.

Scholastic Democracy for Kids
teacher.scholastic.com/scholasticnews/indepth/democracy_plaza
Activities, information, and links about democracy, government, and elections.

National Archives Constitution of the United States
www.archives.gov/exhibits/charters/constitution.html
Text of the United States Constitution as well as images of the actual document.

Library of Congress: United States Constitution
www.loc.gov/rr/program/bib/ourdocs/Constitution.html
Primary documents in American government and other helpful links.

International Center on Nonviolent Conflict
goo.gl/Jjtts7
Information on the anti-apartheid campaign in South Africa and other protests.

U.S. Elections in Brief
photos.state.gov/libraries/amgov/30145/publications-english/USA_Elections_InBrief.pdf
A good overview about how elections work in the United States.

History Channel Civil Rights Movement
www.history.com/topics/black-history/civil-rights-movement
Information and videos about the Civil Rights movement.

The National Women's History Museum
goo.gl/Jz3v6V
An online exhibit of images and information about the women's suffrage movement.

History Channel: The French Revolution
www.history.com/topics/french-revolution
Information and images of the French Revolution.

PBS.org Liberty! The American Revolution
www.pbs.org/ktca/liberty
Information, activities, games, and images to accompany the PBS television series.

Biography of Gandhi
goo.gl/qMLcUl
Gandhi's life, work, and civil disobedience.

Ben's Guide to U.S. Government for Kids
bensguide.gpo.gov/9-12/election
How elections work and federal officials are chosen.

▶ VIDEO LINKS

History Channel: The Birth of Democracy
www.history.com/shows/mankind-the-story-of-all-of-us/videos/mankind-the-story-of-all-of-us-birth-of-democracy

How Do Senate Elections Work?
video.about.com/uspolitics/How-Do-Senate-Elections-Work-.htm

C-Span: The U.S. Constitution
www.c-span.org/video/?194055-1/us-constitution

CNN Video of Tank Man, Tiananmen Square
www.youtube.com/watch?v=YeFzeNAHEhU

RESORCES

⊙ MUSEUMS AND PLACES TO VISIT

National Archives in Washington, DC
700 Pennsylvania Ave., NW, Washington, DC 20408
866-272-6272 ● www.archives.gov
Contains many of the most important documents of American democracy.

The United States Capitol Visitor Center
First St., SE, Washington, DC 20004
202-226-8000 ● www.visitthecapitol.gov
Information about how to visit the U.S. Capitol.

Smithsonian National Museum of American History
14th St. and Constitution Ave., NW, Washington, DC 20001
202-633-1000 ● www.americanhistory.si.edu
The Smithsonian dedicated to American history.

Independence National Historical Park
143 South Third St., Philadelphia, PA 19106
215-965-2305 ● www.nps.gov/inde/index.htm
Independence Hall and other historic Philadelphia sites.

Washington, DC, News Museum
555 Pennsylvania Ave. NW, Washington, DC 20001
888-639-7386 ● www.newseum.org
A museum dedicated to news and reporting, with exhibits that include protest and movements in American history.

⊙ QR CODE INDEX

INDEX

E

Egypt, civic unrest in, 49, 67, 82, 96
elections, 11, 12, 16–17, 19, 20, 37, 38, 49, 70, 75, 95–96, 105. *See also* voting rights

F

Ferguson, Missouri, civic unrest in, vii, 97–98
Franklin, Benjamin, 33, 41
freedom
    of assembly, 3, 17, 18–19, 59
    constitutional, 3, 13, 17–19, 36, 59, 64
    of petition, 3, 17, 19
    of the press, 3, 17, 18, 36, 59, 64
    of religion, 3, 17, 18, 36
    revolution goals of, 29–30, 31, 32, 33
    of speech, 3, 17, 18, 36, 59
French Revolution, vi, 28, 34–36, 42–43

G

Gandhi, Mahatma, vi, vii, 77, 78
globalization, 64, 67
Great Britain
    American Revolution against, vi, 28, 29, 31–33, 41, 65
    Declaration of Independence from, vi, 13, 33
    government of, 9, 10
    Indian independence from, vi, 76–78
Greece, democracy in, vi, 8, 9

H

human rights, 72–85
Human Rights Watch, 79, 80

I

India, civic unrest in, vi, 76–78
IndustriALL, 81–83
injustice, 29–31, 32–33, 34, 36, 39

K

Kemper Rebellion, 34
King, Martin Luther, Jr., vii, 3, 30, 62, 69

L

labor issues
    civic unrest over, vi–vii, 56–58, 59, 67, 80–83
    Labor Day honoring, 58
    labor unions fighting for, vi, 57–58, 67, 81–83
Latin American revolutions, vi, 36–39

M

Mandela, Nelson, vii, 73, 74, 75, 78
media
    civic unrest communication via, 66, 82, 94–103
    civic unrest coverage by, 47, 48, 63, 64, 82, 83–84, 97, 99–100
    election coverage by, 20, 70, 105
    freedom of the press for, 3, 17, 18, 36, 59, 64

Mexican Revolution, vi, 37, 38, 39
monarchies, 9, 11, 35
music, 15, 39, 63, 74

O

Occupy Wall Street movement, vii, 5, 66–67

P

Pakistan, conflict in, vii, 77, 83–85
Parks, Rosa, vii, 2–3, 4, 5, 30, 56
Paul, Alice, 60–61
press. *See* media

R

racial issues, vii, 2–3, 4, 30, 56, 58, 61–63, 69, 73–75, 76, 97–98
representation, lack of, 29–31, 32, 33, 34, 36, 39
republics, 11–12, 38
revolutions
    American Revolution, vi, 28, 29, 31–33, 41, 65
    Arab Spring, vii, 34, 48–49, 67, 82, 96, 102
    French Revolution, vi, 28, 34–36, 42–43
    Kemper Rebellion, 34
    Latin American revolutions, vi, 36–39
    reasons for, 28–31, 32–33, 34, 36, 39